NEW BEGINNINGS

A REFERENCE GUIDE FOR ADULT LEARNERS

FOURTH EDITION

Linda Simon

SKIDMORE COLLEGE

Prentice Hall
Upper Saddle River, New Jersey
Columbus, Ohio

Library of Congress Cataloging-in-Publication Data

Simon, Linda.
  New beginnings : a reference guide for adult learners / Linda Simon. — 4th ed.
    p. cm.
  Includes index.
  ISBN-13: 978-0-13-715230-8
  ISBN-10: 0-13-715230-2
  1. College student orientation—United States.   2. Study skills—United States.   3. Adult
learning—United States.   4. Adult college students—United States.   I. Title.

  LB2343.32.S576 2010
  378.1'98—dc22   2008047541

Vice President and Executive Publisher: Jeffery W. Johnston
Executive Editor: Sande Johnson
Editorial Assistant: Lynda Cramer
Senior Managing Editor: Pamela D. Bennett
Project Manager: Kerry J. Rubadue
Production Manager: Kathy Sleys
Full Service Project Management: Yasmeen Neelofar
Creative Director: Jayne Conte
Design Coordinator: Candace Rowley
Cover Design: Suzanne Behnke
Cover Image: Getty Images, Inc.
Director of Marketing: Quinn Perkson
Marketing Manager: Amy Judd
Marketing Coordinator: Brian Mounts

This book was set in 11/13 TimesNewRoman by GGS Higher Education Resources, A Division of Premedia Global,
Inc. It was printed and bound by Bind-Rite, Robbinsville/Command Web. The cover was printed by Bind-Rite,
Robbinsville/Command Web.

Pearson® is a registered trademark of Pearson plc
Prentice Hall is an imprint of Pearson Education, Inc.

Pearson Education Ltd., London   Pearson Education North Asia, Ltd., Hong Kong
Pearson Education Singapore Pte. Ltd.   Pearson Educación de Mexico, S.A. de C.V.
Pearson Education Canada, Inc.   Pearson Education Malaysia Pte. Ltd.
Pearson Education–Japan   Pearson Education Upper Saddle River, New Jersey
Pearson Education Australia PTY, Limited

Prentice Hall
is an imprint of

3 2280 00996 8892

PEARSON
www.pearsonhighered.com

10 9 8 7 6 5 4 3 2 1
ISBN-13: 978-0-13-715230-8
ISBN-10:   0-13-715230-2

C O N T E N T S

STRATEGIES FOR MANAGING TIME AND STRESS   39

DEVELOPING NOTE-TAKING, STUDYING, AND TEST-TAKING SKILLS   49

STRATEGIES FOR READING   63

STRATEGIES FOR RESEARCH   73

STRATEGIES FOR WRITING   99

GRAMMAR BRUSHUP   115

MATH BRUSHUP 131

FINANCING YOUR EDUCATION 157

s an adult learner and a returning student you are motivated, focused, and eager to succeed. You have decided to enroll in classes to better prepare yourself for the workforce, pursue a new career, or seek advancement in your current career. You may want to complete a degree program that you interrupted to take a job or start a family. As an adult learner, you face challenges different from those of many first-year students who enter college directly after high school. If you've been away from the classroom for some time, you may doubt your ability to succeed at academics. You wonder how you will manage time, hone good study skills, and learn to write successful college papers. You wonder if you will feel comfortable speaking up in class. You wonder if you can compete with your classmates and earn good grades.

New Beginnings is a helpful and reassuring guide to college success that addresses your specific needs as an adult learner and returning student. Since its first publication, those needs have changed and evolved in some areas, and *New Beginnings* has been revised to respond to such changes. In this fourth edition, you will find new information about how to do research using the Internet and how to evaluate Web sources and other resources; how to plan and deliver successful oral presentations; how to work efficiently on collaborative projects; what to expect from online courses and how to evaluate the skills needed to succeed in such courses; and how to find up-to-date information on financial aid.

The eight chapters in this book will help you:

- recognize how your life experiences benefit you as a student
- assess your own strengths as a learner
- choose knowledgeably among course offerings, including online courses
- find the help you need when you need it
- manage time and stress effectively
- learn new study and test-taking skills
- practice new reading strategies
- engage in productive research in libraries or using online sources
- write successful papers

- work on collaborative projects
- make successful oral presentations

In short, you will get the support you need in order to succeed. *New Beginnings* is dedicated to all of my students who have worked so hard to achieve their goals; and to all of the adult learners reading this book, who are returning to school to make a positive difference in your lives.

A CHAPTER PREVIEW

New Beginnings will help you build upon your life experiences and practice the new skills that will help you to become a successful student. Here is an overview of what you can expect from this book.

CHAPTER 1, BECOMING A STUDENT. As you begin or resume your college career, this chapter helps you to identify your strengths as a student, set long-term goals, and learn to feel productive and comfortable in a class environment.

CHAPTER 2, ASSESSING LEARNING NEEDS AND COURSE REQUIREMENTS. Becoming a student means taking responsibility for your own learning. This chapter will give you some guidelines to help you assess your own learning style, establish productive relationships with your teachers, understand a college catalog and course syllabus, and understand degree requirements. It helps you to evaluate your own learning style and to choose appropriate courses. You'll learn the differences between types of courses (seminar, workshop, lecture, online) and find definitions of different disciplines.

CHAPTER 3, IDENTIFYING COLLEGE RESOURCES. Adult education programs often provide a wide range of support services for their students. This chapter outlines and defines those helpful sources so you will know where to find the support you may need during your college career.

CHAPTER 4, STRATEGIES FOR MANAGING TIME AND STRESS. Because adult students need to find time for school in their already busy lives, they need to develop strategies for coping with overload, burnout, and stress. This chapter offers ten hints for time management.

CHAPTER 5, DEVELOPING NOTE-TAKING, STUDYING, AND TEST-TAKING SKILLS. This chapter will help you develop the skills you need to take effective class notes, prepare for and take tests, and understand your grades.

CHAPTER 6, STRATEGIES FOR READING. Reading is the most crucial activity for any course. This chapter offers general rules for reading efficiently and helps you to develop useful strategies for reading a textbook, a theoretical book or article, fiction, and poetry.

CHAPTER 7, STRATEGIES FOR RESEARCH. How do you find information from a library? From the Internet? From interviews? From databases? This chapter gives you the basics of research, including hints for taking notes, documenting sources, and organizing material.

CHAPTER 8, STRATEGIES FOR WRITING. Frequently, writing is the most daunting challenge for adult learners. This chapter guides you through the writing process, offering helpful strategies for generating ideas, drafting, revising, and editing.

APPENDIX A, GRAMMAR BRUSHUP. A quick, painless brushup on the basic grammar you need for editing your own work is found in Appendix A.

APPENDIX B, MATH BRUSHUP. Appendix B is a helpful overview of the skills you need for college math.

APPENDIX C, FINANCING YOUR EDUCATION. A guide to college expenses and different ways to meet those expenses found in Appendix C.

AVAILABLE TO INSTRUCTORS

- Instructor's Manual (online)
- ABC News/Prentice Hall Video Library Series

To access the Instructor's Manual online, instructors need to request an instructor access code. Go to **www.prenhall.com**, click the **Instructor Resource Center link,** and then click **Register Today** for an instructor access code. Within 48 hours after registering you will receive a confirming e-mail including an instructor access code. Once you have received your code, go the site and log on for full instructions on downloading the materials you wish to use.

ACKNOWLEDGMENTS

My thanks to students Jayne Copley, Linda Karlsson Carter, Wendy Beth Russo, Robert Vilardi, Kimberly Parke, Hollis Colby, Robert J. Matthews, Cynthia Fowler, Keren R. McGinity, Clare Keller, and Susan Bell for their helpful responses. Thanks also to my assistant, Lisa Davis, for her creative and efficient help.

   I'd like to thank the following reviewers, who offered valuable feedback toward the development of this book. *For this edition:* Deborah A. Herzog,

Lewis and Clark Community College; Dr. Bethany A. Marcus, Southeastern Virginia Training Center. *For previous editions:* Linda Bush, ITT Educational Services; Anne Hughes, Monroe Community College; and Vonda Lee Morton, Middle Georgia College Tina Pitt, Heald College; Valerie De Angelis, Miami-Dade Community College; Kara L. Craig, University of Southern Mississippi; Glenda A. Belote, Florida International University; John C. Bennett, Jr., University of Connecticut; Nancy P. Thompson, University of Georgia; Rosalie A. Vermette, Indiana University–Purdue University, Indianapolis; Elizabeth T. Tice, University of Phoenix; Ann L. Wolnick, University of Arizona; Charles Dahlstrom, Central Missouri State University; John S. Nichol, Phoenix College; Bruce Thomas, Glendale Community College; Susan Deese-Roberts, University of New Mexico; Kathryn K. Kelly, St. Cloud State University; Cynthia B. Leshin, XPLORA Internet Consulting, Training, and Publishing; Jean Beveridge, Johnson and Wales College; Heather M. Kernen, University of Phoenix; Sandra L. Mickel, Borough of Manhattan Community College; and Cheryl Dorenbush, University of Phoenix.

A special thank you to Don Pierce, Heald College, who wrote the "Math Brushup" in Appendix B for this text.

It's really simple, the reason I went back to school. I wanted to change my life.

Andy Sayles,
student

BECOMING A STUDENT

Y ou may want to make a career change, to learn skills that will help you gain a promotion at work, to enrich your leisure-time experiences, or to complete your education after an interruption. Whatever your goal in returning to school, that goal involves changing your perception of both yourself and the possibilities for your future. Through education, you hope to give a new direction to your life.

Adult learners return to school at different stages in their lives and careers. You may never have attended college, or you already may have experienced some form of higher education. You may decide to go to college after raising a family and working to finance your own children's education. You may log on at midnight to send a completed assignment to your instructor in an online class. You may come to class after a full day's work, after making dinner for your family, or before your night shift at the local hospital. You are mature, you are motivated, and you are busy.

There's one other trait that you are likely to share with other adult learners: You are feeling nervous about the journey ahead. Do you have the ability to do college-level work? Can your experiences outside of school help you succeed in class? Will returning to school be worth the considerable time and expense that you will devote to the effort?

This book will help you to answer "yes" to each of these questions. As an adult learner, you have considerable strengths that traditional undergraduates may not have.

1

In this chapter, you will learn how to:

- assess your strengths
- begin to set long-term goals for yourself
- enlist cooperation and support from your friends and family
- build a good relationship with your instructors
- feel comfortable and productive in class
- see how this book will help you during your college career

LOOKING BACK AND MOVING FORWARD: APPLYING LIFE EXPERIENCES TO BEING A STUDENT

If you visualize the person you were at the age of 18, when many students begin their college careers, you'll see a different person from the one you are today. At 18:

- Your decision to be in school may have been influenced by peer pressure or demands from your family.
- You may have had a support system—such as your parents, school guidance counselors, or other trusted adults—to offer guidance and advice if you had problems.
- Your social life may have competed heavily with your academic work.
- You probably had not yet taken on such adult responsibilities as raising a family, supporting yourself, or paying taxes.
- You had less experience with the demands of the workplace.
- You may not have had a clear career goal.

In contrast, as an adult, you yourself are making the decision to return to school and take on the tasks associated with learning. Most likely, you have had experience in the workplace and/or with raising a family; this experience has helped you to see the *value* of education in daily life. Your life experiences have given you considerable strengths. For example:

- ability to juggle many activities at once
- experience in meeting deadlines
- experience in working collaboratively
- experience in recognizing the complexities of problems

Take a moment to think about how your life experiences can help you in your new role as a student.

Juggling Responsibilities

Barbara is a young mother with two children under four years of age. Barbara completed only one year of college before she married, and years later, she has a goal for herself: When her youngest child enters first grade, Barbara wants to return to the workplace to supplement her family's income. But with one year of college, she feels that she will be at a disadvantage, competing against younger workers with college degrees. Therefore, she wants to earn an undergraduate degree. Although she has tentative plans of majoring in business administration, she is open to thinking about other possibilities. Her goal is simply to complete her undergraduate education.

For the past six years, Barbara has been working at home as a wife and mother, as well as participating in the cooperative nursery school that her older child attends. Juggling activities has been a necessary part of her life. From simple family-related deadlines, such as planning an anniversary dinner for her parents, to purchasing supplies for the nursery school, Barbara learned how to:

- break down big tasks into small, manageable tasks
- use lists, calendars, and planning books to set priorities
- be flexible when unavoidable problems (her son's ear infection or bad driving conditions) interfere with her plans
- take time for rest and relaxation so that she can approach tasks with a fresh mind and spirit

A ssessing Your Strengths

1. What strategies have you used when faced with several tasks that compete for your time?

2. How have you found and evaluated outside opinions to help you solve problems?

3. With whom have you worked collaboratively on problem solving? What strategies have you used to make that collaboration successful? What problems arose?

4. How have you conducted research or found sources to help you solve a problem?

Evaluating Information

Rafael, who has just begun an online adult education program, is the oldest child in his family; his three younger siblings—a sister and two brothers—look to him for guidance in making family decisions. Recently, Rafael and his siblings had to make a difficult decision: whether or not to place their ailing mother in a nursing home.

Because the decision was so emotional for all of the family, Rafael took it upon himself to present information as objectively as possible. He met with his mother's doctor; visited local nursing homes and talked with staff members and some patients; talked with a social worker about possible alternatives, such as a visiting nurse or home health care worker; and talked with a co-worker who had placed her father in a nursing home.

When the family gathered to talk about the decision, Rafael summarized what he had found out. Although the social worker presented a positive picture of home health care, his mother's doctor suggested that Rafael's mother was failing physically and would possibly need emergency care at times. Because the nursing home had its own medical facilities, she would be served better there. The doctor's opinion, then, carried more weight than the social worker's because he could predict his patient's future needs.

The staff at the nursing home wanted to sell the facility's services, so the information provided at the home did not weigh as heavily as testimony from the patients, who generally were happy with their care. In addition, Rafael's co-worker had had a positive experience after she placed her father in the same home. Weighing information allowed the family to come to an informed decision. From the process, Rafael learned how to:

- gather appropriate information from experts
- evaluate the information in light of the experts' special interests
- evaluate the information in light of his family's own needs

Working with Others

Ken works a four-to-midnight shift at his factory job as well as attending classes in an adult education program, so he is rarely home to see his children at dinner or in the evenings. When his wife told him that one of his sons—who just turned 13—seemed to be part of a street gang, he first became angry; then he decided to do something about it. If his son were able to participate in supervised after-school activities, Ken believed that he would not be as likely to get into trouble. His community, however, had no after-school programs.

For a month, Ken spent his days off looking for support for his idea. He spoke with the principal of the local middle school, where his son was in eighth grade, and he spoke with several local ministers. All offered to provide space if Ken could provide the personnel and find funding. Who would supervise the teenagers? Who would pay for supplies and salaries?

Concerned with his son's welfare, Ken developed a flyer describing the problem. The principal offered to distribute the flyer at the school and to call a meeting in the school's cafeteria. Although only a dozen parents showed up for the meeting, four of the parents were willing to work with Ken on the project.

Because Ken was accustomed to working independently on the job, commit-tee work proved a challenge in itself. At first, Ken was afraid that the project would fail just because the committee could not agree on its goals. Then he decided to use the "factory method" of solving the problem by giving each com-mittee member a specific task: to find an appropriate space, to plan a reasonable budget, to investigate sources of funding, and to make a publicity plan for the program.

As the members worked on their tasks, they began to respect one another's efforts and opinions. When the most convenient space turned out to be the school's gymnasium, they agreed that a sports program would be a reasonable beginning for the after-school project. Once they made that initial decision, they managed to work together and started the program within six months. Ken's son was among the first participants.

From his experience in solving a community problem, Ken learned how to:

- articulate a problem to others
- enlist support
- listen and allow others to be heard
- generate support and respect within a group

Researching a Problem

Tony is returning to school with no college experience. After high school, he took a full-time job as assistant to the buyer of a local discount department store and, in five years, moved up to a more responsible position. But Tony wants the opportunity to move even further in business and marketing. He realizes that he needs an undergraduate degree to help him attain his career goals.

Tony's responses to the questions on page 3 focused on his purchase of his first car. Like many 18-year-olds, Tony was obsessed for months with the decision. He spoke to friends, visited used car lots, read magazines that tested and ranked cars, and even spent hours in the library reading some reference books that ranked used cars. By the end of those months, he knew the book value of every car in his price range; he could lecture on the relative merits of various cars. He finally felt that he had enough information to make a decision. When he purchased an eight-year-old Ford Taurus, he knew he had made the right decision.

From this project, Tony learned how to:

- find answers to specific questions from a number of different sources
- select the information that proved most helpful in the decision-making process

The situations that Barbara, Rafael, Ken, and Tony experienced have direct bearing on their work as students. As a student, you will need to:

- juggle class assignments, family life, and your job in order to meet deadlines
- evaluate and weigh information that comes from a variety of sources
- work collaboratively with others in finding information and solving problems
- do research and reading as you fulfill your course assignments

HOW BEING A STUDENT AFFECTS YOUR RELATIONSHIPS WITH OTHERS

Many adult students wonder how their becoming a college student will affect the relationships they have with others, particularly friends, family, and instructors. In the sections that follow, people who have been through the process themselves and who are eager to share their experiences with you discuss this important concern.

Friends and Family Members

Susan Bell discovered that some people she knew did not understand her motivation to return to school, and they made her question her commitment to take a new direction in her life. That questioning, however, only made her more certain that she was making the right decision. "Friends, family, and total strangers may make you uncomfortable about becoming a student," she comments; "they are used to you in a different role. Don't let the guilt trips knock you off course. Some people may be threatened, some envious, some just plain uncomprehending. It is up to you to believe in yourself and what you are trying to accomplish."

There are times when believing in yourself and your goals will not be easy. "As with any life change," Hollis Colby adds, "becoming an adult student requires personal sacrifices because it requires a commitment. In turn, you must become more protective of your time, and this, of course, can pose problems at home. First, you must accept your decision to return to school and make it a part of your life. Second, this helps others to accept the fact that there will be certain times when you need to do things that do not involve them, like study, for example. It is not always easy to make time decisions, but it gets easier as you go. And others tend to become more understanding and sometimes interested, too." You can generate that sense of understanding by sharing your experiences with friends and family.

Another adult student, Robert Vilardi, suggests that you set aside time for classes and studying, just as you set aside time to go to work or to do household chores. Make it a necessity, he advises, and others will begin to see it as an important part of your life. "Find a physically separate space and set a definite time for studying," Robert says. "Treat it like a *business* activity. When you return to your family and work from studying, you'll know that 'school' is taken care of, and you'll feel more relaxed."

Instructors

Instructors find that teaching adults is a refreshing change from teaching traditional undergraduates. As stated earlier: Adults have made the decision to come back to school; they are in class because they want to be there; they are highly motivated; their perspective has been enriched by their life experiences. These important qualities make teaching adults rewarding and revitalizing for instructors.

CLASSROOM PROTOCOL

As soon as you enter a classroom, you'll see that there is no prescribed uniform, no dress code, and no assumptions about what students wear. Some adult students will be dressed in jeans and a T-shirt; others may be wearing the suits and ties or the silk blouses and scarves they have worn all day at work. Even though you might come to class dressed casually, neatness, cleanliness, and appropriateness are important.

Even if there are no prescriptions about dress, however, there are shared assumptions about classroom manners. A classroom, after all, is a small community. Although the instructor is the leader in that community, each student is responsible for helping to make the classroom atmosphere conducive to learning.

Diversity

Academic communities value diversity among students and faculty. Diversity includes race, ethnicity, socioeconomic class, sexual orientation, religion, age, political beliefs, cultural experiences, work experiences, travel experiences, and values. The academic setting encourages respectful sharing of opinions and openness to other people's views. Many people hold stereotypes of others, but the academic community encourages its participants to examine and question those views.

Dos and Don'ts in a Diverse Community

1. Do listen respectfully and allow others to express their views.
2. Don't ask one individual to represent the views of an entire group to which he or she may belong.
3. Do encourage others to participate in discussions.
4. Don't ask anyone to share personal information that he or she may not be ready to share.
5. Do ask questions respectfully.

Key Words in Academia

Throughout your academic career, you'll hear the words *argument* and *critical thinking* in many of your classes. In college, these words have a special meaning, different from their ordinary usage. Neither term has a negative connotation, and neither implies hostility or attack.

Argument refers to an assertion that results from analysis or research. If you argue a point, you make that point and defend it with evidence. If you present an argument in a history class, for example, you might be writing an essay about the causes of the Civil War, based on your readings and research. You will support your ideas with evidence from your sources. Another student may present a different argument, based on other evidence.

Critical thinking means analysis, not negative criticism. When you think critically, you ask questions, puzzle out problems logically, and bring your powers of reason to an issue. College gives you mental tools to hone your ability to think critically and analytically, rather than emotionally or impressionistically. When a professor asks you to write a critical paper on some question, he or she is asking for analysis and not a negative opinion.

PRESENTING YOUR WORK

Written Work

In most courses, written work should be presented in typed (or word-processed) form, double-spaced with one-inch margins, in 12-point (or equivalent) typeface. Papers should be fastened with a staple or a paper clip. Most instructors prefer that pages be numbered. All work should be identified with your name, class, and date. Some students, with access to countless font types and color printers, may be tempted to present work that is graphically inventive and colorful. Such presentations, however, usually are not appropriate at the college level. These are some general guidelines; you'll want to check the course syllabus for each instructor's requirements for presenting your work.

Oral Presentations

In many courses, you may present your work orally; sometimes you will hand in a written version of the oral presentation, as well. Rehearsing your presentation in front of a friend or family member may help you avoid "stage fright" in front of the class. Your teacher usually will provide some guidelines for the presentation, such as length and availability of visual services (video player, computer).

Guidelines for Oral Presentations

- **Stay within the time limit.** Generally, speakers allow two minutes to deliver each printed page of text. If you are not reading a prepared text, time your presentation by rehearsing it—even if you are the only listener.
- **Use a conversational tone.** Speak audibly, emphasize words that are important, and vary your pace, just as you would in conversation. Glance around the room from time to time so that all of your listeners feel included.
- **Practice.** You'll engage your audience more successfully if you make eye contact with them. Rehearsing will help you to feel comfortable with your presentation.
- **Outline.** Speaking from an outline or bullet points will help you to look at your audience rather than printed pages. You might project your outline or bullet points on a screen or chart so that your audience can see the shape of your presentation.
- **Be concrete.** Concrete information engages listeners better than abstractions. Examples and anecdotes usually are more interesting than statistics.
- **Define terms.** Think about what your listeners already know about your topic and what they might not know. Avoid using acronyms (WHO for World Health Organization, for example) unless you first tell the audience what the letters stand for.
- **Use visual aids.** Such materials include handouts, charts, slides, video recordings, and presentation software (such as PowerPoint).
- **Elicit questions.** Invite listeners to ask questions, and leave your audience with questions that your work has generated for you. By encouraging discussion, you actively involve your listeners.

Collaborative Projects

In some courses, students work on projects collaboratively. Collaboration means that each member in a group takes responsibility for part of the project. Collaboration depends on cooperation and dependability among all group members. Sometimes, each member will receive a separate grade based on his or her written work as part of the project; in some classes, the group as a whole receives a grade. Your teacher will explain how collaborative projects are graded in the class.

Guidelines for Collaborative Projects

- **Know the assignment.** Make sure all the members of the group understand the assignment in the same way. If there are questions, check with your teacher.
- **Make a schedule.** Group members will have many obligations—other classes, work, family, or even a social life. Agree on a schedule that will work for everyone and lead to successful completion of the project. Keep a progress report or checklist to monitor accomplishments.
- **Share the workload.** Successful collaboration means that everyone contributes equally. If a member of your group cannot contribute, he or she should consult with the teacher for possible reassignment.
- **Check in regularly.** Meeting in person or by e-mail will help the group share accomplishments as well as problems.
- **"Play well" with others.** Even if one member is clearly more organized or prepared than the others, encourage all members to feel appreciated. Don't allow one group member to dominate discussions or decisions.

LEARNING ONLINE

Besides enrolling in courses on college campuses, many adult learners take online classes where they never actually see or meet their instructor or classmates. Some online classes take place in a virtual classroom, where all students log on at the same time, listen and respond to one another and their instructor, and work on assignments independently. This kind of instruction is called *synchronous communication.* Other online classes are self-paced, where students log on at any time and communicate to class discussions by posting comments on the course site. This kind of instruction is called *asynchronous communication.* Most courses incorporate ways for students to share ideas, such as chat rooms, bulletin boards, or e-mail connections.

Becoming a student in an online course draws on many of the same skills and strengths as being a student in a physical classroom. In addition, however, here are some tips for success in the online environment.

TIPS FOR ONLINE LEARNERS

1. *Do participate.* Just as in a classroom, you have a chance to make your ideas known in a virtual classroom or through bulletin boards, chat rooms, or e-mail. All instructors want their students to participate by sharing ideas with them and with the rest of the class. You will get more out of the experience if you are a lively respondent.

C lassroom Dos and Don'ts

- **Do participate.** When your instructor asks a question, she hopes that students will respond. All instructors want to create lively class discussions, and they welcome your contributions. Some students, especially at the beginning of their college career, hesitate to speak in class. But when you share your perspectives and ideas with others, you help to create a rich learning environment. When you do participate, remember that you are communicating with the whole class, not only with the instructor; the students in the back of the room want to hear your comments, too.

- **Don't monopolize class discussions.** Sometimes, in their enthusiasm for the course, a few students will try to answer every question the instructor asks, comment on everything any other student says, and interject questions or remarks throughout every class. Although instructors appreciate eager and engaged students, they want all of the class members, even those who may be shy and may lack confidence, to feel comfortable about speaking out in class. You can help the instructor by monitoring your own contributions.

- **Do come to class prepared.** Lectures and discussions build on what you have read and written outside of class. You will be a more valuable contributor, and you will learn more, if you do your homework.

- **Don't use class time to discuss personal concerns.** If you need an extension to complete a paper, for example, or if you want to inform your instructor that you will be missing a class, talk to the instructor privately before or after class. On the other hand, if you have a question related to the course material, the syllabus, or the course requirements—if you need a term defined or a concept clarified, for example—*do* ask. It is likely that if you do not understand something, others do not also.

- **Don't be distracting.** In the workplace, you know that staff meetings can be disrupted by a co-worker who spills coffee, whispers to a neighbor, or taps a pencil incessantly while others are trying to talk. A classroom is no different. Don't fidget, eat, rustle papers, whisper, pass notes, or otherwise distract your instructor and classmates. Turn off your watch alarm and cell phone, and make sure that your beeper or pager does not go off during class.

- **Do arrive on time.** You'll disrupt the class if you consistently come late. If you have a problem arriving on time, discuss it with your instructor. If coming late is unavoidable, remove your coat and take out your notebook and pen *before* you enter the classroom, take the first available seat, and make sure you catch up with any announcements that were made before you arrived. If you need to leave early, tell the instructor before class begins, take a seat as near to the door as possible, and put on your coat after you leave the room.

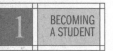

2. *Don't dominate online discussions.* Sitting alone in front of a computer invites some students to digress or pontificate. Remember, your instructor, along with everyone else, is reading your message. Keep it relevant.

3. *Do write in a serious and respectful tone.* Messages to your professor and classmates are different from casual e-mails or text messages. Write in full sentences, avoid slang and colloquial terms, and be aware that your audience consists of a diverse community of learners.

4. *Do be prepared.* Unless you are attending a virtual class, you will need to exert self-discipline to complete assignments and keep up with class discussions. Before contributing to those discussions, make sure you have done the class work.

5. *Do set a realistic pace for a self-paced course—and then keep up with your planned schedule.* Make appointments with yourself to log on at specific times and do your homework regularly.

GETTING YOUR WORK DONE

Whether you work in an office or at home, you've evolved some strategies for getting your work done successfully. Those strategies can be applied to class work, as well.

Set priorities. You've learned how to organize your tasks according to deadlines, ease of completion, and importance. You've learned that if you have a large task to complete, it can be broken down into smaller components. The course syllabus will give you deadlines for work throughout the semester. Keeping a separate calendar for school can help you to break down your work responsibilities into manageable projects. Chapter 4, "Strategies for Managing Time and Stress," discusses setting priorities in more detail.

Organize. You probably have a filing system, a weekly planner, and a daily routine at work. You need a similar system for school. At work, your first task of the day may be to check e-mail and voice mail; at school, your first task may be to check your assignment book and syllabus. Establishing a study routine is as important as establishing a work routine.

Know your responsibilities. Your job description delineates your work responsibilities, and your syllabus tells you your course-related responsibilities. In a sense, the syllabus is like a contract between you and the instructor; it tells you what you need to do to complete the course successfully.

Make informed decisions. At work or at home, you know that the decision-making process involves gathering information and listening to others. Often, you need to seek that information and ask for help. Asking for information and help is not

ommunication and Goals

1. Write a letter to a friend or family member explaining why you want to return to school. As you read the letter, note which reasons seem stronger than others. Why are these stronger?
2. What reactions can you anticipate from the recipient of the letter?
3. How might you meet any objections that the recipient voices?

a sign of weakness, but rather it is evidence of your maturity as a student. Don't hesitate to use the many support services offered through your school. Chapter 3, "Identifying College Resources," discusses support services in more detail.

Identify helpful colleagues. Forming study groups, finding a peer reader for a paper, or just meeting a classmate for coffee to discuss the ideas of the course is a stimulating experience for most students. Some instructors distribute class lists with telephone numbers and e-mail addresses for all students enrolled. In other classes, you may have a chance to work collaboratively with your classmates on some projects. Even if these options are not built into your course, you'll be rewarded by taking the time to establish connections with your classmates.

SETTING GOALS

As discussed earlier in this chapter, adults have many reasons to return to school. Among those reasons:

- to complete an interrupted degree
- to begin a new degree program
- to prepare for a career change
- to learn new skills for career advancement
- for personal enrichment
- for intellectual challenge
- for a sense of community

Just as students differ in their goals, they differ in the time it will take to achieve their goals. Some students can attend school full-time; others can take no more than one course each semester. While some students may complete an undergraduate degree program in a few years, others envision themselves as students for a decade or more. Having a clear sense of your own goals is the first step toward realizing them.

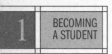

ADDITIONAL RESOURCES

Carter, Carol, Joyce Bishop, and Sarah Kravits. *Keys to Success: Building Successful Intelligence for College, Career, and Life,* 5th ed. Upper Saddle River, NJ: Prentice Hall, 2006.

DiMarco, Cara. *Moving Through Life Transitions,* 2nd ed. Upper Saddle River, NJ: Prentice Hall, 2000.

Johnston, Susan. *The Career Adventure,* 4th ed. Upper Saddle River, NJ: Prentice Hall, 2006.

Whatever subject it is that makes your heart beat faster, keeps you in discussion until 4:30 in the morning, or makes you wake up with a sense of urgency about the topic—that's where you are guaranteed to be successful.

Robert Vilardi,
student

ASSESSING LEARNING NEEDS AND COURSE REQUIREMENTS

eing an adult means taking responsibility for yourself and others; understanding the consequences of your behavior; and learning to act with authority at home, at work, and in the community. At first glance, it may seem that these qualities contradict the idea of being a student: someone who listens, follows directions, and meets other people's requirements. Being a student, however, is not a passive role. As an adult student, you are responsible for creating a plan for learning, seeking help if you need it, and engaging actively in the process of gaining intellectual authority.

Part of that process involves reflecting upon your own learning style, examining your strengths and weaknesses as a learner, and responding to your needs when you create your plan for learning.

In this chapter, you will learn how to:

- understand different learning styles
- evaluate your own learning style
- become aware of your needs as a learner
- choose classes where you can learn most effectively

TYPES OF LEARNERS

In recent years, educators have conducted research on the ways students learn and the strategies that work best for different kinds of learners. Not everyone responds in the same way to reading, listening, studying, and memorizing. Knowing your own learning style can help you devise useful strategies for your own success. In the paragraphs that follow, see if you can identify yourself in one of the three students described.

Visual Learner

Even as a child, Lenny was the kind of student who kept orderly notes and could easily memorize lists of spelling words, definitions, or math formulas. He preferred courses where he could be graded on the basis of short-answer or multiple-choice tests; he felt anxiety, however, about essay questions or term papers. As a reader, Lenny prefers historical narratives that introduce him to people, places, and events that he does not know. He enjoys accumulating knowledge. He likes to do crossword puzzles, but jigsaw puzzles are no fun at all. Lenny:

- is logical and analytical
- is methodical
- concentrates easily
- pays attention to detail
- works well alone

Kinesthetic Learner

Terry calls herself a hands-on person. Her hobby is models—planes, trains, and cars—but she never bothers to read the instruction manual. Instead, she figures out the function of a part by handling it and trying to connect it to other parts. She prides herself on her sense of space and structure. She's the person in her family who gets called on when someone buys a disassembled bicycle or lawn mower. Terry:

- is imaginative and inventive
- is intuitive
- learns through doing
- perceives patterns easily

Auditory Learner

Ted is often the student who talks first in class and eagerly volunteers to give presentations. He is friendly, and if you met him, he'd know your life story in an hour. If he were to tell you, "I know just what you mean," you'd believe him. Once, when he worked as a campaign volunteer for a local candidate, he was given the task of producing an informational flyer about the

EVALUATING YOUR LEARNING STYLE

Circle the letter of the response that most accurately describes you, then see the scoring section that follows to determine your predominant learning style.

1. When I study, I:
   a. can concentrate easily.
   b. get easily distracted.
   c. work best with a study buddy.

2. I prefer an instructor who:
   a. lectures in an organized way.
   b. gives students diagrams or charts to explain material.
   c. allows for plenty of class discussion.

3. If I take an exam, I prefer it to be:
   a. a short-answer or multiple-choice exam.
   b. an essay exam that asks me to draw my own conclusions.
   c. an open-ended essay exam.

4. In taking class notes, I prefer to:
   a. organize the notes as an outline.
   b. organize the notes as maps or pictures.
   c. tape-record lectures.

5. To memorize material, I:
   a. read it over and over.
   b. write it over and over.
   c. say it to someone over and over.

SCORING

If you answered (a) to these questions, your predominant learning style is visual; if you answered (b), your predominant learning style is kinesthetic; if you answered (c), your predominant learning style is auditory.

To further assess your learning style, respond to the following two questions:

1. *List a few of your favorite courses from high school or college.*

   _____

   _____

2. *Identify the courses (such as science laboratories, theater, or physical education) as lecture, discussion, or participation classes. Identify the kinds of tests or assessment you had in each course. Describe the teaching style of your instructor. What conclusions can you draw about your learning style based on your responses?*

   _____

   _____

   _____

candidate's positions. Although he worked hard on the flyer, another volunteer had to complete it because Ted had difficulty organizing the candidate's ideas clearly. Yet when Ted went out to distribute the flyers, he could easily convey those ideas and explain to people how the ideas applied to their own lives. Ted:

- can understand problems and ideas in context
- learns best through conversations
- is interested in other people
- is persuasive
- presents his views easily

Tips for Capitalizing on Your Learning Style

If you are a **visual learner:**

- Underline or highlight main ideas in texts.
- Use flash cards for memorizing terms or facts.
- Create charts or graphs to order information.
- Associate pictures with concepts or facts.
- Choose lecture classes with well-organized instructors.
- Make sure to collect all handouts and study guides.

If you are a **kinesthetic learner:**

- Engage in note-taking while listening to class lectures.
- Translate concepts into maps, diagrams, or action pictures.
- Reword concepts or ideas as action stories.
- Act out ideas.
- Choose workshops whenever possible.
- Look for instructors who provide diagrams and illustrations.

If you are an **auditory learner:**

- Tape-record lectures or class discussions (ask your instructor for permission to do this).
- Read aloud to yourself or a partner when doing reading assignments.
- Study by verbal drilling.
- Choose courses that involve class discussion.
- Take advantage of your instructor's office hours to ask questions or clarify information.

Understanding your learning style can help you make informed choices about classes, instructors, and study strategies. Remember, though, that your own motivation is significant to your success. Although one learning style may predominate for you, you still can be successful in many different courses and class settings with many different kinds of instructors.

ASSESSING
NEEDS   2

UNDERSTANDING CLASSROOM FORMATS

Choosing a particular class depends on your academic goals, the requirements for your degree, and the requirements for your major or particular program. Sometimes, you may choose one class rather than another because the class format fits well with your learning style. There are basically three kinds of classroom settings.

Lecture

In a lecture class, the instructor talks; the students listen, take notes, and usually have an opportunity to ask questions at the end of the instructor's presentation. Lecture classes may range from 20 or 30 students to a few hundred. In a lecture class, students generally are assessed by short-answer or multiple-choice examinations (or, rarely, essay examinations). In a lecture class, you usually are expected to complete reading assignments before class meetings, but you may not receive feedback at each class to help you assess your understanding of the material.

Seminar

A seminar is typically limited to fewer than 20 students. The focus of class time is discussion. Students, then, need to be prepared for each class by keeping up with readings and assignments. Students may be assessed by examinations, by writing a paper, or by completing a project. Because a seminar class is relatively small, there is often significant interaction among the students.

Workshop

Like a seminar, a workshop is a small class focused on both discussion and other classroom activities. Activities include: editing (in a writing workshop); small-group discussions (where students work on problem solving with a partner or a few other students); projects (such as creating a document, report, presentation, or demonstration); and interviewing. A laboratory course in the sciences is, essentially, a workshop course because it provides hands-on learning opportunities.

To assess your own class preferences, complete the worksheet that follows.

ASSESSING YOUR PREFERRED CLASS FORMAT

Write *True* beside the statements that apply to you:

_____ 1. I prefer a large lecture class where I can gather information before I am asked to respond to it.

_____ 2. I prefer a small seminar where I can ask questions as they occur to me and where I can share my ideas with other people.

_____ 3. I am comfortable talking in class.

_____ 4. I like to feel that I have a lot of background before I venture an opinion.

_____ 5. I hate to write.

_____ 6. I read very slowly.

_____ 7. I am afraid everyone else is smarter than I am.

Scoring: If you answered *True* for questions 1, 4, and 7, you may want to begin with large lecture classes, where class participation is not required and where you interact with instructors only through examinations, through writing assignments, or in private conferences either after class or during the instructor's office hours.

If you answered *True* for questions 2 and 3, you welcome interacting with classmates and instructors and want to share the sense of community created in small classes.

If you answered *True* for question 5, you may want to select, among your first courses, a preparatory writing class to help you learn the skills of college writing that you will need throughout your career as a student.

If you answered *True* for question 6, you should monitor the reading requirements for your first courses and, at the same time, inquire about study skills classes in reading that may be offered by your college. Chapter 5 will teach you some useful strategies for note-taking; Chapter 6 will cover reading strategies.

RECOGNIZING DIFFERENT AREAS OF STUDY

What's the difference between American Studies and American History? Between Sociology and Anthropology? In the list that follows you'll find common terms used to describe the various disciplines offered by most colleges.

African American Studies. This interdisciplinary field focuses on the experience of African Americans throughout the American's history. Courses may focus on history, literature, the arts, politics, sociology, and psychology.

American Studies. This interdisciplinary field focuses on the life and culture of the United States. The courses may examine gender, class, ethnicity, literature, history, and the arts.

Anthropology. This field of the social sciences examines human groups and social behavior. Anthropology includes archaeology, which is the study of past cultures and human cultural evolution.

Art. Studio Art gives students an opportunity to engage directly in painting, sculpture, graphic design, or photography. Art History examines the work of artists throughout time and across cultures.

Asian Studies. This interdisciplinary field focuses on the life and culture of China, Japan, India, and other Asian countries.

Biology. One of the life sciences, Biology offers students a chance to explore such topics as plant biology, human biology, genetics, ecology, and physiology through lecture and laboratory courses.

Business. Designed to prepare students to enter the business field, these courses include management, accounting, taxation, organizational structure, finance, and business law.

Chemistry. This field explores the molecular and atomic bases of matter, generally in laboratory courses.

Classics. This field examines the literature, history, philosophy, religion, art, and archaeology of ancient Greece and Rome.

Communications. These courses feature print and nonprint journalism and the role of media in society.

Computer Science. These courses offer the logical, mathematical, and scientific foundations of computing.

Economics. More theoretical than courses offered through the Business department, Economics gives students a background in money and banking, the production and distribution of goods and services, and economic theory.

Education. Learning theory, history of education, and social implications of education, along with courses that lead to teacher certification, are among the areas covered by Education departments.

English. Departments of English offer courses on English and American language and literature, creative writing (fiction, poetry, and nonfiction), and expository writing or composition.

Environmental Studies. This is an interdisciplinary field that combines studies in the natural sciences, humanities, and social sciences, focusing on the life cycles of the natural world, the interaction between humans and nature, and the ethics of ecological decisions.

Foreign Languages. Colleges differ in their grouping of foreign languages. Sometimes a single department oversees all course offerings; sometimes language courses are separated into Romance Languages, East Asian Languages, Slavic Languages, etc.

Geology. Also known as Earth Science, Geology includes laboratory and classroom courses in oceanography, mineralogy, and environmental science.

Government. Also known as Political Science, the field of Government offers courses in American and international politics, philosophy, history, and law.

History. American History and International History often include courses in the history of groups, such as women, African Americans, and immigrants of various ethnic backgrounds.

Mathematics. This field includes statistics, geometry, calculus, algebra, and introductory courses for nonmajors.

Music. Courses offered by Music departments cover music appreciation, history, theory and composition, and performance.

Philosophy. Topics of study include ethics, religion, aesthetics, logic, critical reasoning, and the history of philosophy.

Physical Education. Activity courses give students a chance to engage in sports, exercise, or performance; theory courses introduce students to the physiology of exercise, sport history and philosophy, and nutrition.

Physics. Topics of these courses include gravity, electricity, magnetism, light, and atomic energy.

Psychology. The science of the mind and personality offers courses in theories of personality development, abnormal psychology, ways of learning, perception, and emotion.

Religion. Sometimes included in Philosophy departments, these courses explore the fundamentals of world religions through their various texts, art, and traditions.

Sociology. This social science examines the ways human groups—such as the family or the community—organize, function, and change.

Theater. Courses include acting, directing, voice, set design, playwriting, production, history, and criticism.

Women's Studies. This interdisciplinary field draws upon literature, sociology, psychology, history, and the arts to examine the changing role of women in society.

CHOOSING YOUR CLASSES

Open up any college catalogue and you're likely to feel overwhelmed by the possibilities. A course called *Business Ethics* might help you on your job; a course called *The Arts: Opera* might open up a whole new aesthetic experience. Should you take a course entitled *Organizational Behavior* or *Organizational Change?* What's the difference between the two? What difference can the course make in your new career as a student?

Deciphering Course Descriptions

A catalogue course description is a brief summary designed to help you decide whether you want to register for the course. It is the first step in the decision-making process. As you gain some experience in reading course descriptions, you'll be able to decode them to answer the following questions:

1. Is this a *survey* course?

2. What *prerequisites* or *co-requisites* are necessary? That is, what courses do I need to take before, or at the same time as, I take this course?

3. Is this a *lecture* course, a *seminar*, or a *workshop?*

4. How much writing does this course require? The course description may indicate the writing requirements. Otherwise, visit the department and check the syllabus that the teacher may have on file.

5. Does this course require out-of-class activities or meetings?

6. How does this course fit into my long-range plans as a student?

7. Is this course required or recommended for my major?

8. Is this course one of my electives?

You'll see in your college catalogue that some courses have a description beyond the content of the course. The following will help you understand some of the terms commonly used in describing courses.

Survey. A survey course offers an overview of a large body of material. Typically, students will come out of the course knowing key figures, key terms, and key issues for the course topic. A survey course often serves as an introduction to more focused courses.

The following example is from a college catalogue (New York University):

Literary Romanticism

The genesis and evolution of Romanticism are traced through its literary forms. The course integrates the prose and poetry of Blake, William Wordsworth, Dorothy Wordsworth, Wollstonecraft, Godwin, Percy Bysshe Shelley, Hazlitt, Lamb, Scott, Marx, Carlyle, Lawrence, Goethe, Heine, Schiller, Lessing, Hegel, Sand, Hugo, Stendhal, and Nerval.

The long list of authors covered in this course is your clue that this is a survey course, looking at key British, French, and German writers—novelists,

Identifying Your Course Requirements

Knowing the requirements of your program is an important first step in deciding which courses you will take and in what sequence you will take them. You may want to answer these questions with the help of an advisor or counselor at your school.

1. What courses are requirements for all students at your college?
2. What courses are requirements for all students in your particular degree program?
3. What courses are requirements for all students in your major or concentration of study?
4. What courses are prerequisites for advanced courses in your field?
5. What courses are recommended by your advisor because those courses give good preparation to meet your goals?
6. What courses do you want to take as electives because they fulfill a special interest of yours?

poets, and essayists—during the literary period known as Romanticism. Students will read samples from each of these authors to become familiar with their style and subject matter.

Prerequisite. A survey course is often required to give students a basis for more focused courses. For example, the course *Literary Romanticism* would serve students who want to study nineteenth-century French literature, Wordsworth and his circle, or women and Romanticism.

Even courses that are called *introductions* often have prerequisites. For example (New York University):

Introduction to Investments

Prerequisites: Math I; Principles of Accounting. An introduction to the various types of investments employed by individuals and institutions. The purposes, advantages, and disadvantages of each are discussed. Topics include objectives and methods of investing, short- and long-term planning, forecasting and timing, and kinds of investments (including stock options and mutual funds).

The prerequisites for this course tell you that without a background in basic mathematics, and without the information you would learn from an introductory course in accounting, you will be at a disadvantage in the course. You will not be learning the mathematics and accounting skills you need during this investments course.

Suppose, however, you have been working professionally in billing and accounting. If you think you have the necessary prerequisites because of your life experience, you should contact the instructor to help you assess your background.

Evaluating a Course Syllabus

A course syllabus may be available from the advising office of your college or directly from the instructor. A syllabus is a course plan, including general course requirements, required books, schedule of class discussions, homework and writing assignments, and dates for exams.

Here are some questions to consider as you look at a syllabus.

Questions to Ask About a Course

1. How heavy is the reading load?
2. When are papers due?
3. Am I expected to write papers during school holidays?
4. How will I be evaluated?
5. Are there out-of-class obligations?
6. Does the course seem well organized?

1. *How heavy is the reading load?* A novel a week may be too heavy a load for a slow reader or for a student working long hours. How much quiet reading time will you have to devote to the class? How quickly do you read? With these two figures in mind, you should be able to evaluate the reading load for the course you are considering.

YOUR COLLEGE CAREER PLAN

How close will you be to achieving your goals after five years? Fill in this worksheet with courses that you are taking or that you plan to take this year and in the following four years.

	FALL	SPRING	SUMMER
This year			
Year 2			
Year 3			
Year 4			
Year 5			

_____ Total credits needed for degree or completion of program

_____ Total credits expected to accrue in five years

_____ Credits needed after five years

_____ Expected graduation date

2. *When are papers due?* Compare the due dates with your own work and family obligations. Will you be able to complete the course requirements on time?

3. *Are you expected to write papers during school holidays?* If Thanksgiving means preparing a dinner for 12, you may not have time to produce the paper you need to hand in the following Monday. If Christmas vacation means family and child-care obligations or an increased workload at your job, you may not have time for library research. When are the papers due? When is the final exam? Do those dates give you time to work and study?

4. *How will you be evaluated?* Some courses ask students only for papers. Other courses have a midterm and final exam. Still others ask for class presentations, alone or as part of a group. The syllabus should indicate how you will earn your grade; you can decide if the requirements meet your own learning style.

5. *Are there out-of-class obligations?* Some courses require that you meet with classmates, attend film showings or other events, participate in class trips, or even attend additional lectures. Does the schedule fit in with your free time?

6. *Does the course seem well organized?* The syllabus is the instructor's week-by-week plan of instruction. You should be able to see what topics will be covered in each class, decide whether the topics seem to be ordered logically, and assess whether enough time will be spent on topics that interest you.

ONLINE LEARNING

More and more, adults are enrolling in distance learning programs, where they do not have to travel to a campus or walk into a classroom. Their courses take place online in a virtual community of learners. If you enroll in an online class, you need to have access to a computer, know basic computer and Internet skills, and be self-disciplined. Here are some questions to ask yourself if you're considering taking online courses:

■ **Are you comfortable communicating through writing?** In an online course, you'll communicate with your instructor and other students by writing responses related to the coursework. You need to be able to write clearly and coherently to be a successful online student.

■ **Are you self-motivated?** Most online courses are asynchronous—that is, students log on to the course site and complete assignments on their own time. You may do coursework at midnight or in the middle of the day as long as you can complete assignments when they are due.

■ **Do you have the time?** Logging on to chat rooms or discussion groups is only part of an online course. Your instructor will provide you with a course schedule and assignments, some of which may require hours of reading or research. Make sure you have from 4 to 15 hours a week to complete your work; your instructor may be able to help you estimate the time required for a particular course.

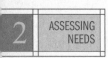

- **Would you prefer a physical community?** Some students enjoy classroom learning because it puts them in contact with other people who share their interests. Online learning sometimes feels a bit lonely to them. Before you choose an online class, ask yourself if you'd rather be sitting next to a real person in a real classroom.

In an online course, your instructor and classmates may communicate with one another through chat rooms or discussion boards. A *chat room* is an interactive site where participants send messages to one another in real time. In an online course, students often respond to an instructor's questions, to students' work, or to class readings by sending contributions to a chat room. Another form of real-time communication is instant messaging.

A *discussion board* is like a bulletin board at a community center or in the workplace, where people post announcements, responses, or items of interest to the community. In an online course, those items of interest will focus on coursework or readings, and students send messages through e-mail for posting on the board. Sometimes, students and the instructor communicate directly through e-mail, without making their contributions available to all on a discussion board.

Finding an Online Provider

Online learning has become a popular form of education. Sometimes, you can find courses offered by local colleges or universities. Even if you take courses online, these institutions may be able to provide you with library resources, advisors, study skills centers, and career offices. If you do not have a local school, or if the courses you want to take are not offered there, Peterson's *Guide to Distance Learning Programs*, updated yearly in print and online, lists accredited learning institutions, their costs, and their programs.

Accredited means that a national or regional certification agency has looked carefully at the course offerings, the faculty, the syllabi, and the educational mission of the program and has approved it. For students who would like to transfer credit toward a degree, to take courses to enhance their career, or to embark on a new career path, it's important that you enroll in an accredited program. Some professions maintain lists of programs that offer accredited courses specifically in that profession.

What You Can Expect from an Online Course

Your instructor will provide a syllabus or course outline, giving a schedule of course topics and sometimes including reading and writing assignments. Some instructors prefer to give assignments as the course progresses. The syllabus should give you information about the basis for your grade: How will your instructor evaluate your learning?

Your instructor will provide a list of readings and source material that may require you to visit Web sites or find material on the Internet. You will also receive instructions about how to communicate with the instructor and your classmates.

You should expect to log on to the course site several times weekly, to keep up with postings on discussion boards or in chat rooms, and to be a responsible and active participant in the class.

S*uccessful Learning Online*

- Make a schedule and keep to it. Keep up with readings and writing assignments, and devote enough time to the class so that you can contribute substantially to online discussions.

- Think before you press "send." Remember: Your readers are members of your class, real people with real feelings. It's easy to respond quickly, especially when you have strong feelings about a question or topic. It's more responsible to think about your ideas and make sure you express them thoughtfully and politely.

- Communicate clearly and correctly. Proofread all of your contributions. Some students recommend reading messages aloud to yourself before sending them to the class.

- Support your ideas with evidence. Make substantive contributions, rather than merely agreeing with others or repeating a comment that someone else made.

- Make your responses concise. If you make notes before responding, you'll find that it's easier to focus than if you simply "think out loud." Conciseness helps your readers to focus on your main ideas.

- Avoid emoticons and acronyms. E-mailing and instant messaging have developed a special vocabulary. :-), for example, means a smile or happiness; BTW means "by the way." But these images and letters may not be familiar to your classmates or instructor. FWIW (for what it's worth), it's better to use conventional vocabulary when contributing to class discussions—BYKT (but you knew that).

ADDITIONAL RESOURCES

The Distance Learner's Guide, 2nd ed. Upper Saddle River, New Jersey: Prentice Hall, 2005.

Peterson's Guide to Distance Learning Programs. www.petersons.com/ distancelearning/.

I just want to tell other students this: There's help out there. Just ask for it.

Allen Jonas,
student

IDENTIFYING
COLLEGE RESOURCES

 ost adult education programs have instituted a wide range of support services to respond to their students' needs. In many programs, students are assigned an advisor to help them choose courses and plan a program focusing on a specific academic discipline. Adult students' needs, however, often go beyond academic advising. Some students, for example, are interested in planning a program that will enable them to make a significant career change; some students have questions about their learning style or a possible learning disability.

In this chapter, you'll see how the following people and services can help you succeed as a student:

- educational advisors
- study skills classes
- instructors
- classmates
- testing services
- counselors for students with disabilities
- career counseling
- personal counseling
- mentoring programs
- tutoring networks

- writing center
- computer center
- librarians

   Information on financial aid can be found in Appendix C, "Financing Your Education."

EDUCATIONAL ADVISORS

Educational or academic advisors can help you plan your program and choose courses that match your background and ability; explain the differences between similar-sounding courses; and share information about an instructor's background and teaching style.

   In some programs, students are assigned an educational advisor as soon as they enroll. In other programs, students seek out academic advisors on their own, whenever they have a question. If you want to find an educational advisor, start first with your school's course catalogue, turning to the section on academic advisement or educational advisement. Unless your advisor has specific drop-in hours, make an appointment: It's not good academic etiquette to drop in on any counselor or advisor.

STUDY SKILLS CLASSES

Many colleges offer classes or workshops addressing such common concerns as how to:

- read more effectively
- take tests
- take better notes in class
- overcome procrastination
- improve memory

   These classes may be taught by advisors, counselors, or professors. They may be offered by an academic department or by your college's learning skills center or office for student services. They may be offered as credit or noncredit courses.

INSTRUCTORS

Suppose your instructor explained the requirements for the next paper in class, but you still have questions about your topic. Or you've been keeping up with homework and assignments, but you still feel nervous about the midterm. Perhaps you've followed the instructor's lectures all term, but suddenly you feel confused by some concepts presented in class.

   If you have concerns such as these, your first source of help is your instructor; don't feel shy about talking with him or her. Instructors know that teaching goes on both inside and outside of class, and they welcome questions from students who want to learn and succeed.

Part of any teacher's job is meeting with students individually; most set aside some time before or after classes to hold office hours—in their office, in the hallway outside of class, or in a local coffee shop. If possible, telephone or e-mail your instructor to set up an appointment to talk during these times. Most professors are eager to help you with class-related questions, something you don't understand from a lecture, an assignment that is giving you trouble, or a deadline you can't meet. You'll find that most instructors are cooperative, interested, and helpful—but you have to seek their help.

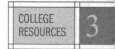

COLLEGE RESOURCES 3

CLASSMATES

Besides your instructor, you may find it useful to talk about the course with your classmates, who are likely to share your doubts and concerns. You'll be less worried and more prepared for examinations, for example, if you form a study group to discuss the material you need to know for the test. Talking about ideas from the course, exchanging class notes, and getting feedback from your classmates make a study group a productive educational experience. Groups should be small—not more than six, most students say—and focused. If you join a group that tends to spend its time gossiping or complaining, don't waste your time.

TESTING SERVICES

Most college campuses offer testing services. Psychological testing can help you assess your learning style or identify a learning disability. Placement testing can assess your level of achievement in such courses as foreign languages, mathematics, or computers.

Some students who have had difficulty with academic work in the past may have an undiagnosed learning disability such as dyslexia (a disability that interferes with the processing of written or spoken information) or a condition such as attention deficit disorder (a disability that makes it difficult to focus on lectures or reading). Learning disabilities do not indicate a lack of intelligence. Testing for learning disabilities is not the same as the intelligence testing you may have undergone as a child. Evaluation for learning disabilities will help you determine whether you have a specific weakness in one or more academic skill areas, including reading, writing, and math. If testing uncovers these or other disabilities, a counselor or advisor can help you learn strategies to compensate for your particular learning needs. You will also discover more about the ways that you learn and process information.

You should not hesitate to arrange for testing. It is always confidential, and most students find that the more they know about themselves as learners, the more power they have to succeed.

COUNSELORS FOR STUDENTS WITH DISABILITIES

3   COLLEGE RESOURCES

Students with visual, auditory, or physical disabilities have special needs and rights. Counselors can help you arrange for many support services, including:

- tutors
- interpreters
- readers
- typists
- physical aides or escorts
- signers
- note-takers
- alternative testing arrangements (e.g., providing for extended time, a non-written format for questions or answers)

You can locate these counselors for disabled students through your educational advisor, office of student services, or office of disabled student services.

CAREER COUNSELING

Career counselors can help you assess ways that your education plan relates to your career goals. You may want to put together a course plan to help you advance in the field in which you now work. You may have decided to change careers and have a new goal. Or, you may want to change careers but need help in defining your goal, assessing your skills and aptitudes, and preparing for a change. Career counselors, besides talking with you about your interests and abilities, may administer personality inventories or tests that help you define your strengths, interests, and personality traits.

Career counselors also can help you write a resume and cover letter, practice for interviews, and assemble a dossier containing letters of recommendation from instructors or employers and other documentation of your abilities (such as artwork, if you are applying for jobs in advertising or design). Career counseling offices may sponsor job fairs once or twice a year, where local companies and recruiters send representatives to talk with students and sometimes to arrange interviews.

In some programs, internships provide both course credit and work experience. Internships are paid or unpaid employment opportunities designed especially to teach students about an industry, company, or profession. Internships are available in both the private and public sectors of employment; they provide a valuable way to introduce students to new job possibilities.

PERSONAL COUNSELING

Besides academic concerns, you may want to talk with a counselor about issues such as anxiety, depression, personal problems, or pressures. Counseling services, located in your college's health center or office for student services, usually provide immediate access to psychologists, social workers, or psychotherapists. These professionals offer short-term counseling and can provide referrals for longer-term support. This counseling is, of course, confidential.

COLLEGE RESOURCES   3

MENTORING PROGRAMS

In some programs, new students are matched with upperclass students or with instructors who serve as guides to the college and the program. If your school has such a service, don't be shy about arranging to meet your mentor and asking questions. Students and faculty members who volunteer to be mentors are knowledgeable about the resources available at your school and are eager to share their experiences and expertise with beginning students.

TUTORING NETWORKS

Typically located in the educational advising office or the counseling office, tutoring networks match students with tutors who can help with a variety of subject areas. Many departments also keep a list of excellent students who are available to tutor others. These tutors often are students who have taken the same course that is giving you trouble and who will be familiar with assignments and requirements. Besides tutoring networks, local high schools and campus student employment offices often have referrals to tutors. When you call about tutoring services, here are several questions to ask:

1. What are the tutor's credentials, previous coursework, grades, and previous tutoring experience? Can the tutor provide you with names of references?

2. What materials will the tutor use? Will the tutor rely on the assigned text, or does he have other materials that may be helpful?

3. How long will the tutor spend with you? Where will the tutor meet you? Can the tutor meet with you at a time and place that are convenient for you?

4. How much does the tutor charge?

M aking the Best Use of Support Resources

"Sometimes a student will ask to come during my office hours," says Judy Miller, a professor of sociology. "He'll walk in seeming very nervous, perch at the edge of a chair, and look at me expectantly. When I ask, 'How can I help you?' he says, 'Well, I just thought I'd check in to see how I'm doing.' So I tell him he's doing fine, ask if he's having any problems, and assure him I'm glad to have him in the class . . . and then he leaves. I never know, really, why these students come, but I guess it meets some need for contact."

For some students, a private conversation with their instructor does meet a need for contact and serves to make them feel more comfortable at the next class. But to make a meeting with an instructor, advisor, or librarian more productive, here are some suggestions:

- **Come with specific questions written down.** You may know exactly what you want to ask, but under the pressure of the moment, you may forget. Write down as many questions as you have, place an asterisk next to the most important questions, and keep that list in front of you during the meeting.
- **Do some homework.** Before you meet with your advisor, be familiar with the information already available in the course catalogue. Before you meet with your instructor to discuss an assignment, read the assignment *more than once*. Before you meet with a librarian, do as much preliminary research as you are able to do on your own.
- **Stick to a time limit.** Instructors, advisors, and librarians do want to help you, but they cannot devote hours at a time to do so. If you think you need to meet for more than half an hour, make sure that your resource person is free to help you for a longer period of time—one hour, perhaps, but rarely longer.

WRITING CENTER

A writing center is a place where students can come with assignments, drafts, or even ideas. You can expect to get useful feedback that will help you revise and improve your work. Tutors at a writing center, though, are not going to proofread or correct your paper. In the first place, that kind of service would be unethical; equally important, the tutors would like to teach skills that will help you to edit your own work rather than edit it for you.

Often, colleges have special writing center tutors assigned to work with students whose first language is not English. Such tutors will help solve some of the grammatical problems that may weaken writing.

COMPUTER CENTER

Many colleges provide computer centers where students may go to write papers and work on other assignments. You may use the computer center to meet class-mates for collaborative work or to log on to Internet resources; in some colleges, the computer center is associated with the writing center to provide peer tutoring. Computer centers also may offer courses on the use of different word-processing programs that may be helpful to you in your college work.

COLLEGE
RESOURCES   3

LIBRARIANS

Class work may not be a problem, but there's a research paper due at the end of the term, and you haven't written one since high school. One excellent resource is a librarian.

Your school library may seem intimidating, with 50-foot ceilings and a complicated online catalogue. But no doubt it's staffed with helpful, knowledgeable reference librarians who want to make your work easier and more productive. Librarians *like* to search for things. They were hired precisely to help students like you, and they will be eager to do so.

Librarians can help you best, however, if they know as much as possible about your needs. If you are seeing a librarian to discuss doing research for a

---

P *lanning a Meeting with an Advisor*

Before you meet with any advisor or counselor, use this checklist to help you focus your meeting and use the time wisely.

1. Write down the most important question that you want answered.
2. Write down all the questions that you want answered. Place an asterisk next to the questions you think are most important.
3. Now rewrite the list, ranking the questions according to importance.
4. Summarize the information that you already know that may answer your questions. Do you want any information confirmed?
5. Prepare a notebook or notepad to record the information you will receive from your advisor. Divide each page into headings that refer to your specific questions. During a conversation, an advisor may answer a question that you have not yet asked; with your notebook ready, you'll be able to record the answer in an appropriate place for future reference.

specific assignment, bring the assignment. If your instructor has distributed a list of suggested books for a research paper, bring the list.

If your library offers orientation sessions, take advantage of this service early in your college career. Knowing your library's resources can be a significant help in many courses.

As you can see, there are abundant resources to help all college students. You should never feel that asking for help is admitting weakness or failure; the truth is quite the opposite. Taking responsibility for your learning includes seeking help when you need it.

ADDITIONAL RESOURCES

Berstein, Alan. *Guide to Your Career*, 6th ed. New York: Princeton Review, 2006.

Eikleberry, Carol. *Career Guide for Creative and Unconventional People*, 3rd. ed. Berkeley: Ten Speed Press, 2007.

When you're back in school, you don't ever kill time. You make it come alive.

Jessie Almardo,
student

STRATEGIES FOR MANAGING TIME AND STRESS

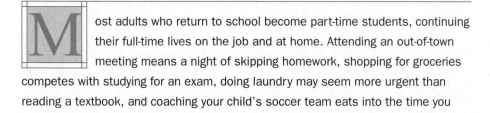

ost adults who return to school become part-time students, continuing their full-time lives on the job and at home. Attending an out-of-town meeting means a night of skipping homework, shopping for groceries competes with studying for an exam, doing laundry may seem more urgent than reading a textbook, and coaching your child's soccer team eats into the time you need to write a paper. If there is one thing that adult students have in common, it's a need to become expert time managers.

Time pressure contributes to many students' feelings of stress—but it is hardly the only cause. Some students feel the pressure to prove themselves in an academic setting; others feel anxious about not having the skills necessary for college-level work. Some students bring stresses from other parts of their lives—family and work, for example—to their college work.

In this chapter, you'll find:

- suggestions for time management
- advice for procrastinators
- advice for perfectionists
- advice on managing stress

TIME COMMITMENTS OF BEING A STUDENT

Attending class is only part of a student's time commitment. Yet even attending class involves more than the one or two hours that the class meets: You may need to allow time for commuting and parking, checking in with your instructor, talking to classmates, stopping to pick up a library book. One class hour, then, sometimes means devoting two or three hours of out-of-class time. And there's more.

Purchasing books and supplies. Before the course begins, allow yourself a few hours to gather the materials you will need to keep up with class readings and discussions.

Reading and studying. For every hour that you spend in class, allow at least two hours a week for reading, studying, note-taking, and review. If you are taking a class that meets for three hours, from 6:00 to 9:00 once a week, for example, you should count on spending an additional six hours in preparation.

Special projects. You may be a fast typist, but writing a college paper involves more than typing: You need to allow time for reading, research, thinking, planning, drafting, and revising. In the week or two before a paper is due, plan on spending blocks of two to three hours for several days.

Special class projects sometimes involve collaborative work with classmates. If such projects are part of the course requirements, allow several two- or three-hour blocks of time for the evenings or weekends when you will meet.

Test preparation. If your course requires a midterm or final examination, allow yourself some two- or three-hour blocks of time during the week before the exam to review readings and notes, learn new material, and memorize information.

TEN HINTS FOR TIME MANAGEMENT

On the next few pages, you'll find ten suggestions from experienced adult students who have faced the same concerns about time management that you likely are facing now.

1. Be Realistic

"My advice comes from my role as an advisor to adults returning to school as undergraduates," says Kimberly Parke. "Do not overestimate your ability to juggle work, family, and school. Do not take on a full-time school program if you are working full-time, never mind if you have a family. Test the waters first: Take one class and work your way up to more classes. This will give you a chance to evaluate the school as well as your own abilities. Don't think, 'Well, it took me ten years to begin my degree, so I want to complete it as soon as possible.' Don't rush through school—it will be at the expense of your job, family, and well-being."

Being realistic also means that you may have to give up a leisure activity, such as a hobby or club, and substitute your classes and homework.

2. Build in "Safe Time"

There are bound to be times when you can't refuse family obligations, when you must work overtime, when you or someone in your family becomes ill, when a snowstorm keeps you from going to the library, or when your car breaks down on the way to class. To avoid panic, student advisor Kimberly Parke counsels students to build in buffers.

Building in buffers means keeping up with—or keeping ahead of—your class requirements. It also means setting aside some flexible time, as Clare Keller has done: "I try to devote certain days of the week to certain aspects of my life in a regular manner and to be as focused as possible on the tasks of each day. But I keep one day unscheduled in terms of outside responsibilities. This is usually my best study day."

MANAGING TIME 4

Susan Bell calls these buffers "wiggle room." "As a television producer," she says, "I got used to handling several different projects at one time. I was always careful to avoid conflicting deadlines and never to promise something unless I was reasonably certain I could deliver. I was also careful to include enough 'wiggle room' to allow for family crises, getting sick, doing the laundry, and the millions of other things that have to be dealt with even if you are a hot-shot television producer. When I could, I would hire other people to do things that I did not absolutely have to do myself. School for me was not much different from television: a lot of projects that needed to be planned and executed more or less simultaneously, with enough breathing room to allow for emergencies and just taking care of life."

3. Keep a Planner

"I used to keep a day planner that was literally my Bible—in size and weight, to say the least," one student reported. "I lugged this tome with me everywhere and had no problems filling up each page (which represented one whole day) with a list of many, many tasks to complete by the end of that day. But I found that I had more space in the planner than I had time or energy in a day. So I purchased a new planner—one as slim as my checkbook—where the week was displayed over two pages. The smaller size forced me to reorganize my tasks so that I spread them out over the week. Seeing how much time I had to fulfill obligations over a week instead of focusing intently on one day not only helped me allocate my time better but eased my anxiety about the amount of things I had to do each day."

4. Find a Space

It can be a real desk in your own study, but just as likely, you'll find that you work at the dining room table or in a corner of the family room. Wherever you work, organize the space to support your efforts. Ask other family members or housemates to recognize your space as yours—at least when you're using that space for your class work.

5. Look at the Big Picture

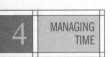

"My advice to new students," says Cynthia Fowler, "is to map out their program of study so that they know their exact graduation date. Holding on to this concrete date can often be a motivator when the task seems overwhelming. As an additional motivator, I kept a small notebook dedicated to charting my progress; at the end of each term, I documented the courses I had completed, checking off degree require-ments fulfilled and generally taking inventory of my accomplishments for that term. I tried to remind myself as often as necessary that if I completed the class I was enrolled in, I would be that much closer to achieving my goal."

6. Speak Up About Your Concerns and Commitments

"The most effective strategy that I developed for time management and organi-zation of work, family, and school has been to communicate with my spouse and to plan ahead," advises Keren McGinity. "For example, I would tell my hus-band about a course, that the syllabus looked a bit daunting, and that I felt anxi-ety about how I would accomplish everything. We would then discuss the upcoming family commitments and ongoing house chores and devise a plan whereby the workload was evenly divided. When I needed to study for an exam or to write a paper, I would tell my husband about it early in the week so that he would know I would be occupied all weekend; we would pick a date in the future when we could spend some quality time together."

7. Work a Little Every Day

You may not have a two-hour block of time each day to devote to studying, read-ing, or writing, but you may have one half-hour—as part of your lunch break, on the bus to work, or after putting the children to bed. Use that half-hour pro-ductively by breaking down a big task into smaller, manageable tasks:

- Review class notes.
- Take notes from assigned readings.
- Make a plan for library research.
- Read a section of a long reading assignment.

8. Make a Checklist Each Week

Each time you can cross off a task, you will feel a definite sense of accomplishment. The key is to keep the list *short*.

9. Just Say No

"Social events must be kept to a minimum, and saying no to invitations by friends was honestly one of the most difficult parts of getting through the program," says Cynthia Fowler. "Like me, most of my friends work full-time, so I did not have the luxury of being in an environment where studying for exams and writing papers were the norm. As a part-time student, I was alone in dedicating my weekends to study and research." That dedication is necessary, though, and so is refusing some—but not all—of the social activities that may have filled your free time.

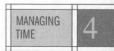

MANAGING TIME   4

10. Get a Study Buddy

Checking in with a classmate before a class meeting may help you both to feel motivated. Because you both are dealing with the same course, you can share strategies for studying, complain about some assignments, and generally cheer each other up. Some students find it helpful to study for exams with a classmate, testing each other on material and sharing notes.

PROCRASTINATION

The procrastinator never does today what can be put off until tomorrow. If you know that procrastination has been a problem in your past academic career, you may want to discuss the issue with an advisor or counselor at your college.

Students often procrastinate when they are afraid of failure: It feels safer not to do the work than to do it and be unsuccessful. Breaking down the study, writing, and review processes often gives procrastinators a feeling of control over the task before them. In Chapters 6, 7, and 8, you'll find the processes of reading, research, and writing broken down into small, manageable tasks so these processes don't seem so daunting.

PERFECTIONISM

Sometimes adult students set impossibly high standards for their own work for a variety of reasons:

- They're paying for their education themselves and feel that earning anything less than an A will make it seem as if they are wasting their money.

- They see grades as justification for their decision to return to school and, therefore, want instructors to confirm their decision with an A.
- They are adults—mature, motivated, hardworking—and believe they should do better than they did when they were younger students.
- They may be older than some of their instructors and equate age with intelligence and ability.
- They know they will share their grades with their companion or child(ren), and they want to feel proud of their achievement.
- They are focused on the product—the paper or exam—not on the process of learning.

Perfectionism is a cause of stress for many students. "The biggest problem I have had as an adult student," Linda Karlsson Carter told us, "has been trying to maintain an unreasonably high standard for my coursework. I wanted to be the perfect student. After two years in school, I decided it was perfectly acceptable to be a B+ student. I knew I couldn't be an exceptional student, an attentive mother, and a productive employee at the same time. When I understood what my priorities were, things began to balance out. I figured I could repeat a course if I failed, but my children would never be 10 and 12 again."

Perfectionism makes it difficult to study and to write. Fear of failure—even if the failure means earning a B instead of an A—gets in the way of learning and can cause continual stress. Perfectionist students are afraid to write (because every word will be judged), afraid to take exams, sometimes even afraid to contribute to class discussions. If being a perfectionist gets in the way of doing your work, talk with a college advisor. Perfectionists may find these tips helpful:

- **Make sure you understand all assignments.** Clarify requirements by asking questions after class, by phone, or by e-mail.
- **Find a peer reader or study buddy.** This individual can help you study and learn class material, discuss your assignments with you, read and comment on your drafts, and so forth.
- **Ask instructors for specific feedback on papers.** Some instructors offer only brief comments about the weaknesses of a paper. If you have specific concerns—about your argument, organization, or particular points—attach a note to your paper when you hand it in. Your instructor's response will help you to improve future papers.
- **Put coursework in perspective.** Besides talking about concerns with a friend or classmate, keeping a journal may help you reflect on your intellectual growth as you move from course to course. A journal helps you to consider all aspects of the course—lectures, writing, talking with classmates, reading—and not to focus solely on the tasks that are judged by the instructor. What about the course is satisfying? Important? Fun?

"I believe the biggest obstacle for a new student is overcoming fear," Linda Karlsson Carter admitted. "I was afraid of failing, afraid I had lost my ability to learn, afraid my family would suffer. Time is the only remedy for fear. I knew that if I continued taking courses, it had to get easier and less stressful, and it did. The only way to overcome fear was to plow right through obstacles. One has to accept that being fearful is a natural part of doing something new; I would rather be fearful than regretful."

"If there is one piece of advice that I would offer to new students, it would be to try to think of everything in terms of *process*," adds Keren McGinity. "It is not as important to get through an exam or to finish a paper as it is to appreciate what you learn either while you are studying or during the research and writing stages. After all, you are doing this for yourself. When preparing to meet with a professor or an advisor, it is easy to dwell on the 'right' questions to ask or responses to give, but it is more rewarding to realize that after the meeting, you will have taken steps toward your goal. In other words, the journey is the most challenging and exciting part, the destination is a by-product. Most importantly: Enjoy it!"

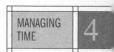

SIX TIPS FOR MANAGING STRESS

Stress does not simply mean being busy, juggling competing responsibilities, or working hard as you strive toward a goal. Stress usually is associated with a feeling of lack of control over one's life. It often leads to physical responses that may involve heart rate, muscle tension, and gastrointestinal problems. Stress often is compounded by feelings of anxiety and sometimes depression.

If stress becomes debilitating and unrelenting, you may want to seek help from a counselor or medical practitioner. Often, however, you can manage stress on your own through some commonsense techniques. Below are six strategies that adult learners have used to help them calm down, cope, and relax. Some of their strategies might be appropriate for you.

1. Identify a Source of Comfort

A cup of tea in the afternoon, a warm bath, or a quiet walk can offer a peaceful break. Take time to read a magazine, or a good book. Play with your dog or your child. Any of these can be a source of comfort and relaxation when you are stressed.

2. Try Relaxation Techniques

Some students find that taking a class in meditation or relaxation techniques helps them. Stress management courses offered through your college, a local hospital, or some health maintenance organizations teach such techniques. Some students find that learning yoga helps.

3. Use Exercise

Most medical practitioners suggest that exercise, as strenuous as possible, often relieves stress. A brisk walk, jogging, aerobic exercise, handball, and tennis all can relieve the tense muscles and nerves that come with feelings of stress. A half-hour of exercise can make your study or work time more productive because you will be able to concentrate better and focus on your work, free from the distractions of stress.

MANAGING TIME

4. Try Imagery

Another stress reduction technique is the use of imagery. Sit quietly in a dark room, close your eyes, and visualize a calming image: clouds, swirls of color, the sea, a field of flowers. Let the image envelop you.

5. Find an Anchor

Anchoring is learning to associate a particular emotional state with a special word or movement. While in a stressed state, recall an experience when you felt relaxed, confident, and powerful. Think of as many details as you can, remembering how you felt at the time. Then choose a word or movement (such as tugging your ear or scratching your nose) to associate with this relaxed state—your anchor. As you visualize your relaxed and confident state, say the special word or repeat the movement that you've chosen. Once you've reinforced the anchor, it should become relatively permanent. When you next feel anxious, use your anchor to remind you of your confidence, self-esteem, and ability.

elaxation Exercise

1. Begin by sitting quietly in a comfortable position.
2. Close your eyes.
3. Breathe in deeply through your nose and feel your stomach (not chest) expand.
4. Continue breathing easily and naturally.
5. Relax your muscles, beginning with your feet and progressing to your face.
6. Picture a calm, relaxing scene.
7. Now put yourself into that scene.
8. Picture someone you trust who believes in you, supports you, and cares about you.
9. Imagine the person is with you and offering you encouragement.

6. Connect with Your Support System

Some students discover that when they return to school, they no longer have time for conversations with good friends. Loss of a valued support system can be a cause of stress in itself. Although you may, in fact, need to cut down on socializing in order to make time for schoolwork, most students advise that you build in time to reconnect with trusted friends.

In this chapter, you've read suggestions by many students who have faced the same feelings of time pressures and stress that you may be feeling. Learning how to manage time and minimize stress is part of the whole learning experience of college.

As you learn new academic skills, the topic of Chapter 5, you'll feel more confident and empowered as a student. In Chapters 6 through 8, you'll find useful strategies for reading a variety of college material, for conducting productive research, and for writing strong papers.

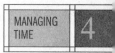

MANAGING TIME 4

Part of what I've learned is *how* to learn.

Patricia Adams,
student

DEVELOPING NOTE-TAKING, STUDYING, AND TEST-TAKING SKILLS

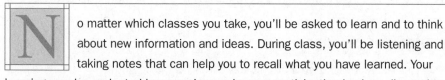

No matter which classes you take, you'll be asked to learn and to think about new information and ideas. During class, you'll be listening and taking notes that can help you to recall what you have learned. Your learning may be evaluated in several ways: by your participation in class discussions, by your written work and projects, and by your performance on tests. At the end of the course, you'll be assigned a grade that reflects your performance. Like many adult students, you may feel out of practice in such academic skills as taking notes, studying, and taking tests.

In this chapter, you'll learn how to:

- take useful notes from class lectures
- study effectively
- take tests with less anxiety
- understand your grades

TAKING NOTES FROM DIFFERENT KINDS OF INSTRUCTORS

In Chapter 7, you'll learn some useful strategies for taking notes from texts and source material. In this chapter, you'll learn some strategies for taking notes from class lectures. The key to taking useful class notes lies in listening: You need to listen for and identify the main ideas that your instructor presents.

As you become a more effective listener, you'll discover that you can identify different kinds of information and ideas from any lecture:

- main ideas, generalizations, laws, or theories
- definitions of key words or phrases
- examples or illustrations of main ideas
- important questions about the topic being presented
- important names, dates, events, places, or other factual information
- bibliography references for further research

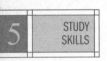

Instructors have different styles of conducting a class. Even in a lecture class, teachers differ in the amount of time they relegate to answering students' questions, the amount of material they note on the board, the number and types of handouts they provide for students, and the way they organize their lectures. In the following paragraphs, you'll read about three different kinds of instructors and learn some helpful strategies for taking notes in their classes.

No matter what kind of teaching style your instructor has, however, it is important that you come to class prepared by completing all assigned readings. If you are familiar with main ideas, key terms, and important questions about the topic of the class, you will be able to listen more productively and take more effective notes.

The Organized Lecturer

The organized lecturer announces the day's topic at the beginning of the class and, during the lecture, writes main ideas on a chalkboard or an overhead projector. At the end of the class, the board contains a complete outline of the main points of the lecture. This kind of lecturer often will emphasize material by offering **pointing phrases**, which are helpful verbal cues (such as "the two main problems," "the four causes of the war," "the most significant source of opposition"). This kind of lecturer often supplies handouts to reinforce class lectures.

TIPS FOR TAKING NOTES

1. Copy all material from the board.

2. Make sure you understand the definition of all key words and phrases that the instructor uses. If you do not understand these terms from the lecture, look for clarification in class readings or ask the instructor.

3. Always be prepared for class by doing reading assignments. The organized lecturer expects students to be organized, too.

4. When studying from class notes, elaborate on the instructor's outline by filling in your own examples and putting ideas in your own words. Your instructor wants you to understand the material presented, not merely reproduce that material on a test.

The Storyteller

The storyteller may be an entertaining lecturer, offering vivid illustrations and examples to help students understand and connect with the ideas of the course. Sometimes, however, students become distracted by the stories told in class and cannot identify the main ideas, key terms, and significant questions of the course.

TIPS FOR TAKING NOTES

1. At the beginning of each class, create your own outline in your notebook. The outline may look something like Exhibit 5.1.

EXHIBIT 5.1   SAMPLE NOTES IN OUTLINE FORMAT.

Topic for this class:

1. First example or illustration: What is the idea behind it?
   a. key word and definition
   b. key word and definition
   c. key word and definition

2. Second example or illustration: What is the idea behind it?
   a. key word and definition
   b. key word and definition
   c. key word and definition

3. Third example or illustration: What is the idea behind it?
   a. key word and definition
   b. key word and definition
   c. key word and definition

2. As you listen to the lecture, remind yourself to ask "What is the point?" or "What am I learning?" as your instructor gives illustrations and examples. What is this story an illustration *of?* What is this example demonstrating? The outline will direct you to answer this question.

3. Ask questions. During the question period or, if necessary, after class, make sure you have filled in your outline to your satisfaction. If not, ask your instructor to underscore the main idea. In an Economics class, for example, you might say, "You told us a dramatic story about a software entrepreneur, but would you just go over the economic principle you were trying to get us to understand?"

4. When you study, make sure you can relate the ideas and definitions given in your textbook or class readings to the examples and illustrations given in class. Make sure, also, that you are clear about the material you are expected to know for a test. Often, the storyteller assumes that you can learn main ideas from the readings and, therefore, prefers to use class time to relate those ideas to real-life situations or to expand upon the examples given in the textbook.

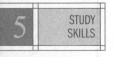

The Discusser

Your instructor may use the **Socratic method** of teaching: asking open-ended questions and eliciting responses from the students. This kind of instructor assumes that students will come prepared by doing class readings and will participate seriously and thoughtfully in the dialogue of the class. If you are used to taking notes only from what an instructor says, you may leave class with only a few sentences. In a class led by a discusser, you need to identify important points made by students, as well. The discusser often will highlight such important ideas by:

- affirming the idea ("Yes, that's right" or "Good, that's a key idea")
- summarizing the idea ("As Carlos said . . .")
- paraphrasing the idea ("Yes, in other words," or "Put another way")
- showing how the idea leads to another idea ("Once we've established this," or "What question does this bring up now?")

TIPS FOR TAKING NOTES

1. Always be prepared by doing class readings, and come to class with your own summary of the important points.

2. Listen for the instructor's cues about the value of ideas discussed. If the instructor highlights an idea, write that idea in your notebook.

3. In your notes, distinguish between a main idea and an example or illustration.

4. Use your notes for recording your own responses to the instructor's questions, even if you don't voice each of your responses in class.

5. When you study, compare the ideas in your class notes with the main ideas and key words from your class readings. How did class discussions expand upon or modify those ideas or definitions?

Exhibits 5.2 and 5.3 show two samples of notes from students in American Literature.

EXHIBIT 5.2   NOTES SAMPLE ONE.

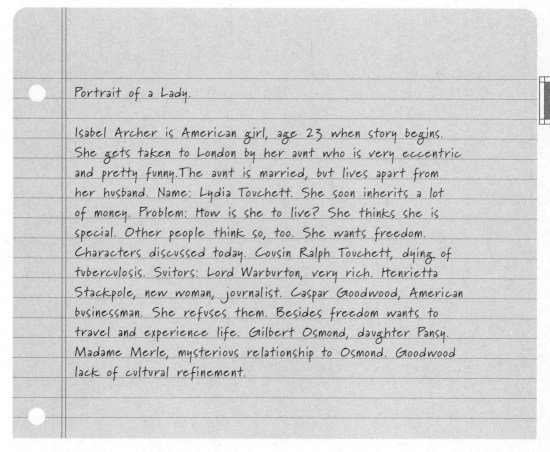

Portrait of a Lady.

Isabel Archer is American girl, age 23 when story begins. She gets taken to London by her aunt who is very eccentric and pretty funny. The aunt is married, but lives apart from her husband. Name: Lydia Touchett. She soon inherits a lot of money. Problem: How is she to live? She thinks she is special. Other people think so, too. She wants freedom. Characters discussed today. Cousin Ralph Touchett, dying of tuberculosis. Suitors: Lord Warburton, very rich. Henrietta Stackpole, new woman, journalist. Caspar Goodwood, American businessman. She refuses them. Besides freedom wants to travel and experience life. Gilbert Osmond, daughter Pansy. Madame Merle, mysterious relationship to Osmond. Goodwood lack of cultural refinement.

As you can see from the first note sample, the student has written down ideas without order and without high-lighting what is important.

Another student used an outline. In the second set of notes, you can see that the student is organizing information in a way that will make it easy to study, to find main ideas, and to distinguish minor points of information (such as Mrs. Touchett's humor) from important information (such as Madame Merle's mysterious qualities).

EXHIBIT 5.3   NOTES SAMPLE TWO.

Portrait of a Lady

I. Characters:
  1. Isabel Archer, American, 23, inherits fortune from uncle
  2. Daniel Touchett, uncle
  3. Lydia Touchett, aunt, who lives apart from uncle
  4. Ralph Touchett, cousin, dying of tuberculosis
  5. Henrietta Stackpole, journalist, friend of Isabel's
  6. Madame Serena Merle, friend of Mrs. Touchett and Osmond
  7. Pansy Osmond, daughter of Gilbert Osmond

II. Suitors:
  1. Lord Warburton, rich British nobleman
  2. Caspar Goodwood, American businessman
  3. Gilbert Osmond, American expatriate, loves art

III. Plot
  1. Isabel inherits money
  2. thinks about the course of her future
  3. has to choose between three suitors

IV. Questions
  1. Why is Serena Merle so mysterious?
  2. Why does Isabel choose to marry Osmond?
  3. What is the function of money as she makes her decision?

eneral Pointers for Taking Class Notes

1. Be prepared with a notebook and at least two pens or writing implements. If you are an auditory learner, ask your instructor if you may tape-record lectures. Even if you record lectures, also take notes.

2. Keep a folder for each class in which you can collect and organize handouts.

3. Choose a seat where you can hear easily and can see the lecturer, the chalkboard, or any visual aids such as an overhead projector or map.

4. Avoid sitting near distractions such as a friend, a window, or a source of noise (such as an air conditioner or heater).

5. Listen for cues from the lecturer. Some lecturers:

    - pause before an important point
    - write an important point on the board
    - repeat an important point
    - make a point, give examples, and then repeat the point
    - change volume or inflection before an important point

6. Summarize rather than attempt to copy every word.

7. Write in outline form rather than in paragraph form.

8. Underline main ideas.

9. Fill in points right after the lecture. While the class is still fresh in your mind, jot down some words or phrases to remind you about the most important ideas of the lecture or discussion and make a note of material to reread or study. If you have a tape recorder, make verbal notes of ideas to study or to follow up in your reading.

10. If your instructor tells you that certain material will be tested, make sure to identify this material by starring, underlining, or highlighting it.

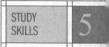

STUDY
SKILLS   5

As soon as possible after class, take a look at your notes and answer the following three questions:

1. What is the most important idea I learned from class today?

2. What are three important terms I learned to define or understand?

3. What question do I want to answer (either from class readings or the next class discussion) to help me understand the material?

Responding to notes soon after class helps to reinforce what you have learned, provides an orientation for the next class, and helps you when you study from your notes to prepare for a test.

HOW TO PREPARE FOR TESTS

Besides writing papers, tests are the source of greatest anxiety for all students, adults included. Preparing for tests is a two-part process: assessment and study time.

Assessment

There are basically three kinds of tests:

1. Multiple-choice

2. Short-answer

3. Essay question

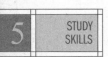

Sometimes, instructors will combine these forms of testing, asking you to complete 50 multiple-choice questions and answer two out of three essay questions, for example. Because the form of test will affect your study plan, be sure to ask your instructor to explain the test in as much detail as possible. Many instructors set aside time to discuss a test a few weeks before it will be given. Be sure you know the answers to these questions:

- What kind of test will be given: multiple-choice, short-answer, essay question, or a combination of these?

- How long will you have to complete the test? Is the test given during class time, or is there a longer period of time allotted for the test?

- Is the test an open-book test? An open-book test allows you to bring texts, readings, and lecture notes for reference during the test. Although you can bring such materials, you still need to know the course material thoroughly.

- Can you bring a dictionary to class? Especially if English is not your native language, a dictionary may help you to express yourself clearly and correctly.

- What material will the test cover: the entire semester, the last few weeks, or a particular unit of study?

- What sources will the test cover: textbook, lectures, outside reading?

- What sources does the instructor think are most important?

- Are old tests available for use as practice?

- What might a typical multiple-choice question look like? A typical short-answer question? A typical essay question?

- What is the purpose of the test? Is it to see how well you have memorized key terms? To see how well you synthesize ideas presented throughout the semester? To see how well you can develop your own analysis or argument about the issues of the course? Knowing the purpose of the test can help you to anticipate the kinds of questions that will be asked.

Study Time

Test preparation begins when you take notes in class and from assigned readings. When you take notes, make sure that you define key terms as you go along. Chapter 6 (on reading) and Chapter 7 (on research) will give you some useful strategies for taking notes. If your notes are clear and well organized, they will be useful for test review. If you have missed any class lectures, it's a good idea to get notes from a classmate whose work you respect.

Some students find that if they prepare for a test too far in advance, they forget what they have memorized; a week's intensive review is more helpful. Other students find that several weeks of studying and review plant ideas and concepts firmly in their memory. Whatever study schedule you choose, remember that cramming the night before the test is a poor strategy. You'll arrive at the test exhausted, anxious, and unfocused. Reviewing the night before, however, can refresh your memory and leave you feeling more confident.

STUDY SKILLS 5

Some students find it helpful to study with a partner or in a group. Study groups can be useful if they are focused on reviewing material rather than on open-ended discussions, complaining, or worries. If you form or join a study group, make sure the other members are people whose work you respect and who have kept up with assignments and attended lectures. Study groups should meet several times before a test and set a clear agenda for each meeting.

Preparing for a Multiple-Choice or Short-Answer Test

Multiple-choice and short-answer tests draw upon your ability to define terms and distill concepts into a few words or phrases. The key to studying for these tests is memorization. One way to memorize is to *write down key words with a short definition.* Using 3×5 index cards is a timeworn strategy to help you memorize key terms. On one side of the card, write the term; on the other, write a brief and precise definition. A multiple-choice test will try to trip you up by offering a definition of a term that is similar to the correct definition but is worded in a way that makes it incorrect.

If your textbook lists key words as part of a chapter review, make sure that you transfer all of these words, with their correct definitions, to your index cards. If your instructor has used key terms in class lectures, make sure these terms also are among those you learn. As you are studying, if you find that you need clarification of certain terms, be sure to ask your instructor.

If you are an auditory learner, you may want to work with a study buddy so that you can repeat key words and definitions aloud; then listen as your partner does the same. Using a tape recorder may also be an effective study tool for an auditory learner.

If you are a kinesthetic learner, you may want to write and rewrite key words and their definitions. You also may want to associate words with images or action as much as possible. Visualizing terms as part of a picture, image, map, or structure may help you to remember them.

Preparing for an Essay Test

If your textbook has questions as part of a chapter review, one option for study is to *write answers to the questions and keep track of the length of time it takes you to answer them.* Part of the skill of taking an essay examination is being able to answer questions adequately within the time limit of the test. The more practice you do before the test, the more quickly you can respond to questions and the more successful you will be.

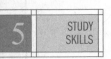

If your textbook does not have a chapter summary, ask your instructor for a few examples of essay questions. These examples should give you an idea of what your instructor is looking for: summary of specific readings, synthesis of several readings and class discussions, analysis of a text, or your own argument based on readings and class material. Once you have these questions, write answers to them.

If getting sample essay questions is not possible, you can formulate your own by turning topic sentences from chapters or sections of chapters into questions.

For auditory or kinesthetic learners, it may help to first discuss your responses with a partner or study buddy. As you talk, take notes to help you write an outline for an essay response; then write the response, being sure to keep track of your time.

TEST-TAKING

Get a good night's sleep, eat something before the test (but not so much that you'll feel sleepy), and arrive a few minutes early. Bring to the test everything that you need: pens or pencils, calculator, and books (if the test is an open-book test). Wear a watch or sit in a place where you can see the clock. Take a deep breath; then follow these eight steps:

1. Look over the test before you begin.

2. Make an estimate of the amount of time you will need to complete each section of the test.

3. Begin with multiple-choice or short-answer questions, answering those you're sure of and placing a dash or dot next to those you are not sure of.

Types of Essay Questions

Your instructor asks you to respond to essay questions in order to see how deeply and thoroughly you have thought about the course material. Rather than test your ability to memorize facts and information, the essay question tests your ability to analyze source material or synthesize what you have read. In general, essay questions fall into five categories. Understanding the purpose of each kind of question may help you be more successful in responding:

1. **Agree or disagree.** This question gives you a statement by an expert. Using readings and class notes, you formulate an argument agreeing or disagreeing with the expert. Don't be afraid to disagree. If no disagreement were acceptable, your instructor would not give you the question.

2. **Support a generalization (or a theory) with examples.** This question gives you a statement by an expert. Using class readings and notes, you are to provide examples to show that the statement applies to specific events or ideas you have learned about in the course.

3. **Analyze a text.** Usually, this question will ask you to focus on what meaning is conveyed by a text (poem, essay, story, work of art or music, etc.) or how the text achieves its effect. You will be expected to apply the strategies of analysis that you have learned during the course.

4. **Make a comparison.** This question asks you to look at two or more texts, events, thinkers, or ideas and show some important similarities or differences among them. As in all essay questions, you want to focus on specific points to make the comparison. When you answer this question, you may discuss first one text and then another, or you can set up an outline point by point, returning to discuss each text as you move through the points of comparison.

5. **Put a text, event, or idea in context.** This question asks you to show how a text you have read for the course fits into a larger social, historical, cultural, or artistic context. In answering this question, you want to define the context in as much detail as you can; then you specifically show how the text, event, or idea responded to or grew out of that context.

STUDY SKILLS 5

Sometimes, answering the questions that are easier for you acts as an on-the-spot review, helping you to recall more information.

4. Go back to the troublesome questions. In a multiple-choice test, eliminate the obviously incorrect choices and then make the best choice from whatever remains.

5. Assess the essay questions. How much time do you have for each one? Again, begin with the easiest question, making it clear in your response booklet exactly which question you are answering.

6. Write an outline. Begin by responding directly to the question in a sentence or two. Then, make a list of at least three concrete points that will support your answer. Students often lose credit on essay questions because they repeat generalizations rather than refer to specific material from readings or class lectures.

7. Organize the outline. Make sure that the three points you make are logically connected.

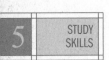

8. Write or print legibly.

UNDERSTANDING YOUR GRADE

The grade you receive for a course reflects the quality of your work, not the quality of you as a person. It is not a reflection of how much the instructor likes you. Getting a low grade in one course does not mean that you have no ability to continue as a student; getting an A in a course does not mean that you can expect to get an A in every other course you take. These statements may seem commonsensical, but it's likely that you'll reread them several times during your college career. Getting a grade means being judged, and being judged is not easy for anyone.

Instructors often include criteria for grading in their syllabus or set aside a few minutes of class time to discuss grading policies. In general, teachers consider the following five criteria in grading:

1. Test scores

2. Grades on papers

3. Class attendance

4. Quality of class participation

5. Extra projects

Different instructors weigh these criteria differently, placing more or less emphasis on test scores or participation, for example. You should understand your professor's criteria for grading in each course you are taking.

At the end of the semester, if you receive a grade that is a surprise to you—usually because it is lower than what you expected—you may want to contact your instructor so you can understand how the grade was computed and learn what you can do in another course to improve the quality of your work. You may find that you have evidence to dispute the grade, and sometimes an instructor will agree to change a grade.

The following, however, are *not* reasons to dispute a grade:

1. *You worked very hard.* Remember that the grade reflects the work you produced, not the effort that you put into that work. In a difficult course where material is unfamiliar, you may have to work much harder than in a course in your field. Still, you are not being graded on effort, but on the products that result from that effort.

2. *You need the grade to keep up your grade point average (GPA).* Sometimes, your admission to a degree program or your standing in a program depends on your maintaining a certain GPA. Sometimes, your employer will reimburse you for tuition if you earn a high enough grade. Your instructor, however, is not responsible for that GPA or your employer's tuition policy—you are. Take the opportunity to find out how you can improve rather than dispute a grade that you earned.

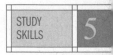

STUDY SKILLS 5

3. *The person who sits next to you got an A, and she's no smarter than you.* Remember, the grade reflects your work, not your general intelligence or aptitude. Many factors can influence the quality of your work, some course-related (you missed a few lectures), some personal (you had unusual family responsibilities during the semester). Your classmate may have been better prepared for the course than you because she took a few other courses in the department.

If grading causes unusual anxiety for you, you may want to seek help from your academic advisor or personal counselor. Everyone would like to earn an A in every course; not everyone does.

The next several chapters, like this one, focus on the skills you need to do your best in all of your classes.

ADDITIONAL RESOURCES

Carter, Carol, Joyce Bishop, and Sarah Lyman Kravits. *Keys to Effective Learning,* 4th ed. Upper Saddle River, NJ: Prentice Hall, 2005.

Carter, Carol, Joyce Bishop, and Sarah Lyman Kravits. *Keys to Success*, 5th ed. Upper Saddle River, NJ: Prentice Hall, 2006.

Hancock, Ophelia. *Reading Skills for College Students*, 6th ed. Upper Saddle River, NJ: Prentice Hall, 2004.

Holschuh, Jodi, and Sherrie L Orist. *Active Learning: Strategies for College Success*.

LearningExpress. *Math Skills for College Students*. Upper Saddle River, NJ: Prentice Hall, 1998.

LearningExpress. *Vocabulary & Spelling Skills for College Students*. Upper Saddle River, NJ: Prentice Hall, 1998.

Majors, Randall E., and Joan Marie Yamasaki. *Is This Going to Be on the Test? And Ten Other Questions That Can Save Your College Career*, 3rd ed. Upper Saddle River, NJ: Prentice Hall, 1997.

Ooten, Cheryl and Emily Meek. *Managing the Mean Math Blues*. Upper Saddle River, NJ: Prentice Hall, 2003.

Pauk, Walter. *How to Study in College*, 8th ed. Boston: Houghton Mifflin, 2004.

Wong, Linda. *Essential Study Skills*, 3rd ed. Boston: Houghton Mifflin, 2000.

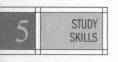

5   STUDY
SKILLS

The main part of intellectual education is not the acquisition of facts
but learning how to make facts live.

Oliver Wendell Holmes, Jr.,
Supreme Court Justice

STRATEGIES FOR **READING**

 n most of your college courses, you are likely to be assigned many different kinds of reading material: textbooks, theoretical books and articles, critical books and articles, fiction, plays, and poetry. In college, all of these various kinds of reading materials are called texts. Based on these texts, you may be asked to:

- memorize information
- respond to an author's arguments or analysis
- develop your own questions about the material presented
- use the readings as a basis for writing assignments
- show your understanding of the readings on examinations

Reading course material is different from reading the morning newspaper, an office memo, or John Grisham's latest thriller. College texts may be more difficult to understand; you have to *learn* as you read, not just come away with vague ideas. You have a responsibility to process and think about what you read; in the end, your course grade may depend on your skills as a reader.

This chapter offers you some strategies for honing those skills, for becoming an active reader. You'll learn strategies for:

- reading actively
- reading a textbook
- reading a theoretical or critical book or article

- reading fiction
- reading poetry

TAKING AN ACTIVE APPROACH TO READING

Simply put, an **active reader** responds to texts. This means an active reader:

- takes notes
- asks questions
- discovers patterns
- looks for main arguments
- thinks about how evidence supports an argument

Active reading, then, is different from the kind of reading you may be accustomed to doing. It takes more time, more concentration, and more skill. Here are six general guidelines for becoming an active reader:

1. Read in a quiet place.
2. Be comfortable—but not so comfortable that you'll fall asleep.
3. Keep note-taking materials at your side.
4. Keep a dictionary handy.
5. Remember that reading an hour every day is more productive than reading for several hours at once.
6. Set aside a few minutes of every reading period for review.

READING A TEXTBOOK

Introduction to Economics, American History, Principles of Literary Theory: The titles of textbooks announce that they convey essential course information. Textbooks, which are the main reading material for many courses, offer a special challenge for any student. There seems to be so much information that it's hard to know what is important and what is not. What will appear on a test? What is necessary to remember? Here are some strategies for making textbook reading more successful.

Get oriented. Like other books, textbooks are organized into chapters that present information on various topics. Unlike other works of nonfiction, though, textbook chapters themselves are organized into sections that focus on specific areas of information. This structure is designed with learners in mind: Textbook authors want to present material in manageable amounts to help you assimilate it as easily as possible. Looking at the structure of a chapter is the first step toward learning the material.

Here, for example, is the organization of a chapter from *Fundamentals of Investing*, an introductory textbook used in a business course:

Chapter title: Investment Markets and Transactions

Section 1: Securities Markets
Subdivisions: Types of Markets
                Organized Securities Exchanges
                The Over-the-Counter Market
                NASDAQ
                Regulation of Securities Markets
                General Market Conditions: Bull or Bear
Section 2: Making Security Transactions
Subdivisions: Stockbrokers
                Basic Types of Orders
                Basic Types of Transactions
                Transaction Costs
Section 3: Summary
Section 4: Key Terms
Section 5: Review Questions

READING   6

The structure of a chapter gives you a useful outline of the information presented and provides a map to guide you through the material you need to learn. In *Fundamentals of Investing*, as in many other textbooks, the authors provide a summary of main points, a list of key terms, and questions to help you test your knowledge of the material.

Read and write. Some students read with a highlighter, turning their black-on-white textbook into a rainbow of yellow and pink. In fact, for kinesthetic learners, highlighting in different colors is a useful strategy for identifying key terms or ideas. But highlighting alone leaves out an important processing step: your own summary, in your own words, of what is important.

Reading with a pen and index cards (or a notebook) may be a bit slower, but it will be more efficient in the long run. As you read, summarize, and write, you are processing information and producing a useful study tool for examinations and paper writing.

Skim as you go. You don't have to read every word of every chapter. You do, however, need to read and understand key definitions and main points. Here, for example, is a section from *Fundamentals of Investing*. As you read this paragraph, think about what is important to note:

The risk of not being able to liquidate an investment conveniently and at a reasonable price is called *liquidity risk*. The liquidity of a given investment vehicle is an important consideration for an investor who wishes to maintain flexibility in an investment portfolio. In general, investment vehicles traded in *thin markets*, where demand and supply are small, tend to be less liquid than those traded in *broad markets*. However, to be liquid an investment must be easily sold at a reasonable price. One can generally enhance the liquidity of an investment merely by cutting its price. For example, a security recently purchased for $1,000 would not be viewed as highly liquid if it can be sold only at a significantly reduced price such as $500. Vehicles such as bonds and stocks of major companies listed on the New York Stock Exchange are generally highly liquid, whereas others, such as an isolated parcel of raw land in rural Georgia, are not.

This paragraph defines *liquidity*. In your notes, you would include that definition, but you would not necessarily include the information given after the words "for example". If you understand the definition of liquidity, then this part of the paragraph can be skimmed.

Look for definitions and blocks. Graphics are an important textbook feature. Key words and definitions often are italicized or printed in boldface; important concepts often are separated from the rest of the text in shaded or framed blocks. Memorizing definitions is an easier task when you have created your own flash cards from the textbook or, if you are an auditory learner, when you have recorded key words and definitions into a tape recorder.

Ask questions. Textbooks convey information in the form of statements or assertions. When you frame those statements as a question, you take a useful step in the process of reviewing. Here are three questions you might ask after reading the paragraph on liquidity:

1. What is liquidity?

2. Why are some investments less liquid than others?

3. How can an investment be made more liquid?

Your instructor might ask questions like this in class or on an examination. When you formulate questions as you read, you will feel better prepared for both experiences.

Review. Build in a review period—10 or 15 minutes—every time you read. You can review by skimming a chapter and looking at the topic headings for each section, or you can review by looking at your notecards. Reviewing each time you read will make preparing for examinations much more efficient.

READING A THEORETICAL OR CRITICAL BOOK OR ARTICLE

A theoretical or critical book or article gives you an author's interpretation or argument about some topic. A literary critic may show you a new way of looking at a novel or short story; an economist may offer a way of interpreting recent market trends; a historian may offer a perspective on interpreting events of the past.

Criticism, as academics use the term, does not mean a negative assessment of something. In ordinary conversation, if I criticize your cooking, I may be pointing out its shortcomings. But when scholars *criticize a text*, they analyze it and interpret it. If you are studying *Hamlet* in a literature course, for example, your instructor may ask you to read a critical article or book interpreting the meaning of the play or the behavior of the characters.

The steps of active reading apply to a theoretical or critical book or article, as well as to a textbook.

Get oriented. An active reader of a theoretical book or article looks first for the author's main idea. In a book, this idea will be presented in the preface, fore-word, or introduction. In an article, the main idea appears in the first few paragraphs. The preface to a book or the beginning paragraphs of an article offer a useful guide to the rest of the text, helping you to understand:

- the author's motivation in writing the text
- the sources to which the author will refer and the evidence the author will use
- the problem the author wants to solve

READING   6

Read and write. As you read, respond to the author's assertions in marginal notes, in a note-book, or in a reading journal. Keep in mind that the author is a real person writing to you, a real reader. Your comments and marginal notes, then, become part of a conversation that the author began by writing the text.

Some students find it helpful to write a "letter" to the author, after reading a text, summarizing the main ideas, responding to points with which they agree or disagree, and asking questions. This "letter"—not sent, but used as a study tool—is one strategy of an active reader.

Skim as you go. Thinking about the author's aims and intentions will help you to connect with important ideas in the text. Once you identify the author's main argument, you can construct your own outline of the supporting assertions or main points. These assertions usually are developed in clusters of paragraphs— similar to the subsections of a textbook—that support the assertions with evidence and examples. As you gain experience reading a theoretical or critical text, you will be able to identify more easily the beginning of each cluster of paragraphs.

Look for definitions. The author's argument depends on *key words* defined and explained within the text. You know that you have found a key word when it recurs throughout an argument and when the author defines or discusses its meaning.

As you read a theoretical or critical book or article, you may encounter either unfamiliar terms or words you know used in an unfamiliar way. Here, for example, is a passage from "*Dracula*'s Backlash," a critical article about Bram Stoker's famous novel, *Dracula*:

> It is certainly true that Dracula, the narrator's pivotal vampire, is a male, but the world in which he operates is a world of women, the world of Eve, a world in which reversion and acculturation are at war.*

Among the difficult terms in this passage are: *pivotal, reversion, acculturation.*

What do these words mean? Sometimes, it is possible to deduce the meaning from the text. *Pivotal*, you might guess, means crucial or important; calling Dracula the *pivotal vampire* implies that there are other vampires in the novel, but he is the most important. Even if you did not guess the meaning quite accurately, since *pivotal* serves only as an adjective, its importance in the sentence is minor compared with nouns and verbs. But *reversion* and *acculturation* are more difficult terms and, as nouns, apparently more important. If you have a dictionary beside you as you read, you would want to stop here and make sure you understand the meaning of these words.

Ask questions. Here are ten questions that will help you to connect with the author's aim:

1. What is the author's main point?
2. What problem or question does the author consider?
3. Whom is the author addressing? Who is the audience for this text?
4. What assumptions does the author make about the reader?
5. To what extent does the author want to change the reader's way of thinking or acting?
6. What is the author's tone in this text: Informal? Conversational? Friendly? Distant?
7. What words, phrases, or images recur throughout the text? How do these words, phrases, or images help to fulfill the author's purpose?
8. How has the author's analysis changed or enlarged your understanding of the topic?
9. What point(s) do you agree with? Why?
10. Where do you disagree? Why?

Review. Build in time to take one last look at your notes. Have you given yourself a sense of the structure of the argument and the author's main points? When you look at your notes, do you discover a place where you explain the author's main point?

*Bram Dikstra, "*Dracula*'s Backlash," In *Dracula: A Norton Critical Edition*, eds. Auerbach and Skal. New York: Norton, 1997: 460.

READING FICTION

In such courses as literature, women's studies, and even history, works of fiction—novels and short stories—often are assigned as texts. Fiction offers a different kind of reading experience from textbooks or theoretical and critical texts. When you read a story, it may seem that there is nothing more to say about it than to describe what happened to which characters. Your instructors, though, will be asking you to analyze these texts, not merely to summarize them.

A summary, however, is a useful first step after reading a fictional text. In a summary, you condense the plot and give brief descriptions of the characters. While writing a summary, you may think of questions that you want to ask about the author's choices in creating a text: Why is one character angry? Why is the story set in the Australian outback? Why does the main character seem so self-destructive?

After you have written a summary of the text, you are ready to move on to analyzing the text. The following 12 questions will help you think about fiction in a deeper way than you may have approached such texts in the past.

1. What events in the story are most significant? Why?
2. Who are the main characters? How would you describe the personality traits of each?

3. How do these characters change?
4. What do the characters learn?
5. How does the author make you care about the characters?
6. Where does the action take place? What is the setting?
7. How does the setting relate to the plot? To the characters?
8. Who is narrating the story? What is the relationship between this narrator and the other characters?
9. What is the relationship between the narrator and the author?
10. What problem does the author present in the text? What main idea does the author explore?
11. What images recur throughout the text? How are they important?
12. How does the author's style help you to understand the problem or main idea of the text?

Questions such as these—and you will invent some of your own—help you move from merely telling what the story says to exploring how the author communicates with you, the reader.

READING POETRY

Poetry is a particular form of creative writing that some students find difficult to read. Certainly, one of the main features of poetry is that it is elliptical: Words are deliberately omitted so that a poem does not read like a sentence. Poems, however, can be exciting puzzles to figure out; they can provide rich reading experiences.

Here are eight questions to help you discover the meaning of a poem:

1. Who is the speaker in the poem, the poet or someone else?

2. Who is the intended audience for the poem?

3. What problem or issue is the poet exploring?

4. What images, words, or phrases recur throughout the poem? Why does the poet emphasize these images, words, or phrases? How do they relate to the meaning of the poem?

5. What sounds are repeated or emphasized in the poem? Why?

6. What is the form of the poem? Does it have stanzas? Does it have a regular rhyme scheme? Does it have a regular rhythm? How does the form relate to the meaning?

7. What feeling or emotion does the poem evoke in you? Why?

8. What images or words in the poem stand for other ideas? Why did the poet choose these particular images or words? How are they effective?

Practice applying these questions to the following short poem by American poet Emily Dickinson:

My life closed twice before its close

My life closed twice before its close—
It yet remains to see
If Immortality unveil
A third event to me

So huge, so hopeless to conceive
As these that twice befell.
Parting is all we know of heaven,
And all we need of hell.

Source: Emily Dickinson's poem "My Life Closed Twice Before Its Close."

It's easy to see that Dickinson is writing about death, but what is her point? Here are some questions that one student asked as he read the poem:

■ How do we experience death before we actually die ourselves? What possible experiences might Dickinson have had that were huge and hopeless?

Analyzing Your Reading Assignments

After completing a reading assignment, use this list to analyze what you've read.

1. What is the main idea of this text?
2. What words cause difficulty in comprehension? List those words, look up their meanings, and record the definitions.
3. What are the author's key words? List them and write a brief definition for each.
4. Identify the most important passages. Why do you think these are important? Write a brief explanation.
5. Write several questions in response to the text.

- Dickinson mentions heaven and hell: How does she understand these two "places" that figure in Christian religion?
- Why does she emphasize the word *parting* by placing it at the end of the poem and relating it to heaven and hell?

In response to these questions, the student wrote the following paragraph interpreting the poem:

READING   6

> Physical death is the most final experience of separating one human being from another, but it is not the only experience. Emily Dickinson sees any kind of parting—one person leaving another—as a death experience. She tells us in this poem that she has had two such experiences. Separation, maybe abandonment, makes her feel that her life has closed. We do not know what she believes about the possibility of heaven as a reward or hell as a punishment. For her, both "places" are evidence only that the departed person is no longer with her, and so in a sense both places are equal in not being able to soothe her pain.

Although Dickinson's poem is short and fairly self-explanatory, the student who wrote this interpretation read the poem several times before really understanding it.

Reading is the most basic academic skill that you will need to master. In this chapter, you've learned six strategies for becoming an active reader:

1. Get oriented.
2. Read and write.
3. Skim as you go.
4. Look for definitions.
5. Ask questions.
6. Review.

As you apply these strategies to different courses and different texts, you are likely to discover an improvement in your ability to read productively.

To learn is a natural pleasure, not confined to philosophers, but common to all men.

Aristotle

STRATEGIES FOR RESEARCH

 research paper gives students a chance to go beyond the boundaries of the assigned course material, to formulate an interesting question, and to answer that question by reading or consulting various source materials. Those source materials might include books or articles found in a library; information found on the Internet; interviews; films; television programs; and works of art, music, dance, or theater.

A research paper, however, is not merely the kind of report that you may have written in high school. In college, a research paper (just as any other college essay) involves interpretation, analysis, and argumentation.

In this chapter, you'll learn how to:

- choose a topic for research
- formulate a question
- define your terms for online searches
- practice Internet search strategies
- evaluate Web sites
- take notes
- document sources
- organize notes
- avoid plagiarism and overdocumentation

CHOOSING A RESEARCH TOPIC

A **topic** names the area of interest that you want to pursue in your paper. In a philosophy class, a topic may be an abstract term, such as morality or ethics. In an accounting class, a topic could be the impact of tax law on financial planning. In an art history class, a topic might be as broad as American Impressionism or as narrow as Winslow Homer's early works.

Finding a topic sometimes seems daunting: If you are very much interested in a course, you may have trouble narrowing down your interests; if you are cool toward a course, you may have trouble coming up with a topic that excites you. In either case, however—and in all cases in between—finding a topic results from active thinking. When you take notes in class and as you read, use the opportunity to jot down questions as they occur to you. When you think about the implications of what you are learning, you'll find that questions are bound to occur to you. What issues or problems puzzle you? What are you curious about?

Topics often arise from personal interests. In a course called *The City in America,* one lecture focused on the ways that immigration changed the housing needs in some major urban centers. A student whose grandparents had been immigrants was curious about his own family's experience. He decided to investigate the topic of immigration and city planning for his research paper. Another student in the class, who happened to be a single mother, decided to research the topic of women workers in cities.

Choosing a topic, however, is only the first step in the research process. A topic does not provide enough focus for a college essay. Writing about women workers in cities, for example, could be the focus of an entire book. Once you have a topic—a subject area that you want to research—you need a focused question that will narrow down the topic to make your research and writing manageable.

7 RESEARCH

FORMULATING A RESEARCH QUESTION

To write a good research paper, you will need more than general ideas on a broad topic. Your paper should be grounded in concrete information that will bring your topic to life and convey its flavor and immediacy. A specific focus in your research will lead you to such concrete information.

If you are having trouble achieving a specific focus, ask yourself questions about your topic. What do you want to know about your topic? The student interested in immigration and city planning, for example, needed to write a ten-page research paper. The topic, of course, was much too broad for such a small paper. To narrow down the topic, the student asked six key questions:

1. Who? (Who are these immigrants?)

2. What? (What kind of community did they create in their new place of residence?)

3. Where? (In what city did they settle? Where in that city did they go?)

4. When? (When did they come?)

5. Why? (Why did they choose that particular city?)

6. How? (How did the city adapt to their presence, and vice versa?)

These questions helped the student to limit the topic to a workable focus for a research paper: How did city planners in Portland, Maine, respond to the arrival of Irish immigrants in the middle of the nineteenth century?

Posing a similar series of questions, the student who decided on the topic of women workers also formulated a focused question: How did the city of Toledo, Ohio, respond to the needs of women workers in the 1950s?

You can see that the focused questions of these two students are of the right breadth for their papers: The students will be able to provide well-researched and precise answers to their questions. But there is more to a good question than its size. A good question also generates your interest as you do research, and your readers' interest as you translate your research into an argument. Good questions have *significant* answers—reasons why your readers should care about your topic.

A good way to ensure that your question is significant is to ask yourself why you are interested in answering it. Will you provide a new way of looking at a particular historical event? For instance, the student writing on nineteenth-century Irish immigration in Portland can provide a unique perspective by discussing his own grandparents' experience. Will you convince your readers that they are involved in your topic in some way? A student writing on a new lunch program in the Boston public schools can suggest the implications of new nutrition research for us and our health. Doing research will help you to appreciate and articulate the significance of your topic.

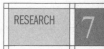

DISTINGUISHING PRIMARY AND SECONDARY SOURCES

Research papers are based on two kinds of sources: primary and secondary. A **primary source** does not contain someone else's interpretation of the material; rather, it may be a novel, a work of art, economic statistics, laws, maps, letters, or a film, depending on the research topic.

Suppose, for example, that you are writing a research paper about the economic conditions of farmers in Connecticut at the end of the nineteenth century. A diary kept by a farmer would be a primary source. Billing records from a local supply store would also be a primary source, as would photographs, letters from farmers to their relatives, and nineteenth-century newspaper articles relevant to farm issues. All of these sources would provide evidence that you, as the researcher and writer, have to interpret and analyze.

Secondary sources are materials that offer interpretation or analysis of primary sources. Biographies, histories, literary criticism, art criticism, and economic analyses are all secondary sources. For the paper on economic conditions of nineteenth-century Connecticut farmers, for example, a history of Connecticut would be a secondary source. A scholarly article about farm life in the *New England Quarterly* also would be a secondary source.

Secondary sources can help you discover background material, find references to relevant books and articles, and learn how scholars use evidence. In your own paper, however, you must make sure that your argument is supported by evidence from primary sources—that you don't just repeat the arguments you find in secondary sources.

Both primary and secondary sources are important in a research paper, and they are easy to locate once you understand how to look for information in libraries or online.

USING THE INTERNET FOR RESEARCH

The Internet has been described as a "network of networks"—a universe of information sources connected in cyberspace. You can access vast amounts of information on the Net; much of it is organized in ways you will find helpful. For instance, if you have a defined research interest, you can consult sites at which in-depth specialized knowledge is available by subject. If, on the other

hand, you are still trying to settle on a topic, the Internet offers plenty of opportunities for following links from one subject to other related subjects until you find something that really interests you. You can find just about any information you want on the Internet, and the sources of information are not limited to American or English ones, as your library's reference books often are. The Internet is global, which means you can obtain news and publications in foreign languages and from any region on earth where the Internet exists.

The World Wide Web is not the same as the Internet; it is a facet of the Internet, the one you will use the most in research. The Web is a system of sites or home pages that provide links to other pages. These links are in the form of "hyperlinked" (often underlined or highlighted) text, images, or icons. By clicking on one of these links, you can move from site to site as you do research.

One caution about Internet research: Be wary of unreliable information. Anyone with Internet access can post something—anything—on the Net. If no source is listed for a piece of information you find on the Net, try to find out where it came from by querying the Web site by e-mail. If you can't find the source, don't trust the information.

Another drawback of the Internet is that even documented Web sites often contain abbreviated information. For instance, there is a company that publishes reference books on American doctors and hospitals; it has a database on the Internet that contains all of the information appearing in the reference books. However, there is *also* a site on the Web for this company—but it does not contain all of the information that appears in the reference books, so the unsuspecting researcher may consequently miss crucial information. Likewise, older materials are often not available on the Internet: You can get this week's issue of *The New Yorker*, but for an article written in that magazine in 1967, you'll have to go to a library.

Nevertheless, the Internet and the World Wide Web can be important sources. If you are not familiar with using these sources, it may be useful for you to take one of the many orientation courses offered. Your college is likely to offer such courses through the library, the technology center, the computer laboratory, or other such support services.

Evaluating Internet Sites

Because anyone can mount a Web site, users need to evaluate the reliability of sources. The most reliable sources are hosted by a reputable institution such as a college, museum, or professional organization rather than a single person. The most reliable sources are designed for educational, rather than entertainment, purposes.

Here are some questions to help you evaluate an Internet site:

RESEARCH 7

- What does the domain tell you? The domain name is the group of letters after the dot. Common domain names are
    com—a commercial site hosted by a profit-making business
    edu—an educational institution, such as a college or university
    gov—a government organization
    org—a nonprofit organization or business
    net—a network
    mil—military
    uk—a site originating in the United Kingdom
- Who is the author of the Web site? Is the site hosted and managed by an individual? If so, what affiliation does this individual have? If the site is hosted by a group, what authority does the group have to offer information?
- Who is the intended audience? Does the site address children? High school students? Advanced professionals?
- How reliable is the information? What evidence does the site offer to support assertions and claims?
- How current is the information? Often, a site will let you know when it was last updated. Sometimes, currency of information (about political issues, for example, or scientific research) will be relevant to your research.

Internet Lingo

Here are a few terms you should understand in order to do research on the Internet.

- **Telnet.** This is a program that lets you log in to a remote host computer on the Internet and run programs resident on that host computer. Telnet, therefore, is a service that can connect your computer with hundreds of host computers. Your library may provide Telnet to connect with other libraries around the world.

- **Browser.** A browser allows you to view World Wide Web documents. Browsers provide a way to navigate the Internet by pointing and clicking on text or icons. Netscape Navigator and Microsoft Internet Explorer are common examples of browsers.

- **Search engine, search directory.** These are tools to help you find information on the Internet. Examples of search engines are Librarian's Index, Alta Vista, Infoseek, Excite, and Lycos. Examples of search directories are Google, Yahoo!, Magellan, Galaxy, Excite, and Infoseek. Besides these information-finding tools, there are also Internet collections, which are subject directories of Internet resources compiled by individuals. Such directories may focus on archaeology, art, mathematics, government, history, literature, and so forth.

Here are three useful Web sites with links to most online libraries:

http://sunsite.Berkeley.edu/LibWeb
www.metronet.lib.mn.us/lc/lc1.html
http://library.usask.ca/hywebcat

- **Discussion group, newsgroup (Usenet), chat group.** Discussion or chat groups should not serve as your principal sources, but they are useful for finding leads to other sources. Different groups emphasize different issues or topics; if you subscribe to a particular group, you can receive e-mail—relevant articles, transcripts, etc.—on its topics.

Two Web sites can help you find Usenet newsgroups:

www.deja.com
www.tile.net

Some organizations and publications have their own groups. If you go to the address of any group and log in, you can "talk" to other people who are also connected, and thus issue a question to the world at large. You may need to leave your e-mail address and just wait for responses, or you may be able to read all the messages directly on the group's site. For example, National Public Radio's afternoon talk show "Talk of the Nation" has a chat group where you can "converse" with other listeners about the topic being discussed on the air.

Two Web sites can help you find mailing lists:

www.tile.net/lists
www.liszt.com

ONLINE SEARCHES

To find information on the Web, you'll use a search engine, such as Google. Most likely, Google is familiar to you if you've shopped online, looked for helpful tips about anything from symptoms of illnesses to gardening, or planned a trip. Google is not the only search engine—other popular search engines are yahoo.com and ask.com; whichever search engine you choose, the process is the same.

Let's follow a search for research about women's roles on farms in nineteenth century America. To begin, you would enter a few **key words**: *women, farm,* and *nineteenth century.* Key words are terms that a search engine will use to find sources. You might have entered other related terms: *agriculture, female,* and *1800s* for example. You'll see, as soon as you press *search*, that you come up with hundreds of thousands of results. It would be a daunting task to sort through all of them; usually in a search, the first dozen or so are sufficient to provide some useful sources.

With so many apparently relevant references, how can you decide which ones might be helpful to your research? First, spend a few minutes examining where the reference comes from by looking at the *domain name.* The domain name is the identification that comes after "www." In one reference that emerges from this search on Google or Yahoo!, you'll see the domain name *connerprairie.org.* "Org" signifies a nonprofit organization, such as a museum.

Generally, sources hosted by an educational or nonprofit organization are more reliable than sources from a commercial site. If you click on the link for the *connerprairie.org* reference, you'll find an essay about farm women's roles in the late nineteenth century. But from the essay, you still won't know what *connerprairie* is. For that information, you need to click on "Home," to discover that Conner Prairie is a history museum in Indiana. Knowing where your source originates is the first step to deciding on its usefulness.

RESEARCH   7

Some references you may find come from a source identified as JSTOR.org. This source contains references to articles in the humanities and social sciences from many scholarly journals and books. The difference between scholarly publications and popular magazines is a process of selection called *peer review.* This means that other scholars read the essay before it is accepted for publication and decide that it is sufficiently important and well written to deserve being published. Books published by academic publishing houses (Oxford University Press, Harvard University Press) go through the same peer review process.

Using the key words mentioned earlier, you are likely to find a reference to the book *Bonds of Community: The Lives of Farm Women in Nineteenth Century New York* by Nancy Grey Osterud. This book may be in your college library, or it may be available on loan from other libraries through a service called *interlibrary loan.* Your college reference librarian can help you make a request. Since this book is directly relevant to your research, you'll want to look at its bibliography to see what sources the author used. One way to build your own bibliography is to check sources in useful books and articles.

A library online catalogue entry for *Bonds of Community* looks like this:

Author:	Osterud, Nancy Grey, 1948-
Title:	Bonds of Community: The Lives of Farm Women in Nineteenth-Century New York/Nancy Grey Osterud.
Publication Information:	Ithaca: Cornell University Press, 1991.
Description:	ix, 303 p. : ill., map ; 25 cm.
Notes:	Includes bibliographical references (p. 289-295) and index.
LC Subject(s):	Rural women —New York (State) —History — 19th century. New York (State)—Rural conditions.
Record number:	ocm22004130
Call Number:	HQ1438.N57 O88 1991

It's useful to look at the Library of Congress (LC) Subject terms for this source. Using *rural women* or *New York (State)—Rural conditions* as key words can help you as you proceed in your research. If this book proves helpful to you, other books and articles that emerge from a keyword search of these subjects also may be helpful. Also, online catalogues allow you to search for other books at the same Call Number. Clicking on HQ1438.N57 O88 will show you other titles that are adjacent to this one on your library's shelf.

Others references from an internet search might lead you to the following kinds of sources:

- *com* in the domain name refers to a commercial site. Although designed to publicize a business or sell merchandise, a commercial site still may offer interesting material or links to educational sites. You need to be careful, though, because material on commercial sites generally does not undergo a peer review process.

- *edu* in the domain name refers to an educational site. These sites may lead you to libraries, collections, or archives, which may contain manuscripts, letters, unpublished material, or, in the case of nineteenth-century women, newspapers and magazines from the period. Sometimes, archives can provide photocopies of some of their holdings for students who are engaged in research. Clicking on the link can tell you about the collection, whether it is accessible, and how to find out more information.

■ *Amazon.com* frequently appears in searches, leading you to references for books published on your topic that can be purchased through the online bookstore. These titles, though, may be in your library, or you may request the title through interlibrary loan.

ARTICLE DATABASES

Databases in your library may provide indexes and full texts for journal articles, abstracts, reports, and other material in various fields of study. Libraries can subscribe to hundreds of online databases. Some databases are devoted to a single discipline, like PsychLIT for materials written in the field of psychology. Others are multidisciplinary, like Lexis (or LexisNexis), which assembles news pieces from hundreds of papers and journals. Examples of databases that are available at most large libraries are ERIC (Educational Resources Information Center, for material in the field of education), MLA Bibliography (Modern Languages Association Bibliography, for material on linguistics, literature, and languages), and PAIS (Public Affairs information Service, for government documents and policy periodicals).

Databases also offer you access to abstracts, full-text articles, and images in journals, archives, and other collections. An *abstract* is a brief summary of a longer work, such as a scholarly article or research report. The abstract will contain a full citation for the longer work so that you can locate it in a library or, if the service is available to you, request the longer work from your library's Interlibrary Loan Office. Some databases contain links to full-text articles, so that you can download the article from your own computer and print it out. Databases also may contain links to sources of current or historical images. Hundreds of databases cover a wide range of topics. Your instructor often can recommend databases that are best for your research. As in an Internet search, you can use key words to find references and sources.

S ome Useful Databases

Ebscohost.com

Access to a collection of databases for the humanities, social sciences, behavioral sciences, business, educational literature, environmental sciences, and other fields.

ARTstor.org

Access to images of paintings, photographs, and other art forms.

Search.eb.com

Encyclopedia Britannica. Although Wikipedia is a popular source for succinct entries identifying people, places, ideas, and things, the Encyclopedia Britannica continues to be a professional, reliable source of information.

LexisNexis.com

Access to a number of specialized databases focused on education, business, law, and news.

WorldCat

A library catalogue that can tell you where in the world you can find a book you are looking for.

LIBRARY RESOURCES

Once you have a topic and a focused question, you are likely to head to a library to begin your research. Depending on your topic and question, use the following good research sources.

Dictionaries

The range of dictionaries goes far beyond the familiar *Webster's* or *American Heritage*. The *Oxford English Dictionary (OED)* is a multivolume resource that offers historical information on word usage. When is the first time that the word *multicultural* appeared in print? What is the origin of the word *thing?* You can find the answers to those questions in the *OED*. The OED also has an online site at www.oed.com.

In addition, there are specialized dictionaries for science, business, biography, and many other fields. Dictionaries are useful as a first step: They help you to define terms and find basic information about your topic.

Encyclopedias

7   RESEARCH

Just like dictionaries, encyclopedias may be all-inclusive *(Britannica, Americana)* or specialized. The *Encyclopedia of Philosophy,* for example, contains entries, written by experts, on major philosophers and philosophies. The *Encyclopedia of American Industries* contains summaries of hundreds of important industries, offering basic factual information for each. Wikipedia is an online encyclopedia that has generated controversy about its reliability. If you find information on Wikipedia, it's best to compare it with a generally accepted source such as the *Encyclopedia Britannica* or scholarly encyclopedia.

Popular Magazines

Magazines can be important sources of information. But how do you find an article pertaining to your topic? One of the many online or print guides to periodical literature can help you. The *Reader's Guide to Periodical Literature* is widely used and available in many public libraries, as well as in college libraries. When you look up key words for your topic or question, you'll find an entry that gives you the author, title, magazine name, publication dates, and page numbers for an article that may be useful to you. This reference source will help you find information published in such popular magazines as *The Nation, Ladies Home Journal,* and *Reader's Digest.*

Professional and Scholarly Journals

Specialized guides to articles in professional and scholarly journals include the following:

- *Education Index*
- *Art Index*
- *Business Periodicals*
- *Humanities Index*
- *Index to Legal Periodicals*
- *Social Sciences Index*
- *Applied Science and Technology Index*
- *Public Affairs Information Service Bulletin*
- *Essay and General Literature Index*

Most scholarly journals are now referenced in online databases.

Dissertations

Doctoral dissertations that are not yet published as books can be valuable resources for research. To locate a dissertation pertinent to your topic and question, there are several sources you can consult. Among them are the *Comprehensive Dissertation Index, Dissertations in English and American Literature,* and *Dissertation Abstracts International.*

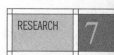

Book Review Digest and *Book Review Index*

This source contains excerpts from reviews of many popular books published in the United States. If you want to quote from a book review, you need to find the review in its original source. Do not quote directly from the *Book Review Digest* because entries offer only summaries of longer reviews; these summaries are not considered a scholarly resource. The *Book Review Index* can be found online for reviews published after 1965.

Biographical Indexes

Biographical indexes offer information on well-known or influential people, past and present. Some indexes, like the *Biography Index,* refer you to other sources of information about prominent people. Others, such as *Contemporary Authors* and *Modern Scientists and Engineers,* offer biographical accounts, which vary in length according to the index. *Current Biography* includes both references to other sources and biographical information. Biographical indexes are generally multivolume series of books, arranged alphabetically by name or profession, which are updated regularly. Usually, an index series has a separate cumulative index volume.

Newspaper Indexes

Newspaper indexes offer complete citations, by subject and author, to news articles. Many major newspapers, including *The Los Angeles Times* and *The Christian Science Monitor,* have their own indexes of articles. *The New York Times Index* is one of the largest and most consulted of these newspaper indexes. *The National Newspaper Index* is a larger index, available on CD-ROM and online, which compiles citations to many newspapers. *LexisNexis* is also a usual database for news articles.

Online Catalogues

In many libraries, an online catalogue contains information on a library's own holdings. This sort of database—generally called an online catalogue—is an updated version of the old-fashioned card catalogue. In card catalogues, the library's holdings are arranged by author, subject, and title. Online, you can do all three searches in one place; in addition, you can conduct searches by publisher, key word, and other features. The online catalogue will produce a list of all the works in the library that match the search word you enter. You can view the long display for each work or choose only those you really want to see. At some computer terminals, you can print the information that appears on screen and take it with you when you search the library shelves.

Both card catalogues and online catalogues provide complete bibliographic information on the library's holdings (one minor difference is that a work's title is sometimes abbreviated in online catalogues). A listing from either sort of catalogue will include the title, author(s), edition, publisher, city of publication, date of publication, total number of pages, number of illustrations (if any), the size of the book (in cm), subject headings, Library of Congress catalogue number or other identification number, and the work's call number and location.

Online catalogues have several advantages. They are continually updated, so you can find out immediately whether and when the work has been checked out and when it is due back. They also include key words and suggest related subjects, which you can search using particular search commands. Some online catalogues allow you to check the book out by computer, using your student ID number. In most online systems, the screen will display a list of possible commands that are fairly self-explanatory, which you type or select. The list should include a "help" command, which will give you specific information on how to operate the search system.

CD-ROM

Most university libraries and larger public libraries have computers on which you can conduct research by CD-ROM. CD-ROM is a way of storing vast amounts of information in very limited space: Information, organized into databases, is stored on CDs, which you "play" in a computer disk drive the way you'd play a music CD. Some disks contain bibliographic information—indexes of titles, authors, and so forth—which directs you to other resources in the library. Some disks have summaries of articles and other written material. Still other disks contain the written material itself that you are looking for—the full text of an article, for instance. Most of the reference publications listed above are available on CD-ROM.

Doing research by CD-ROM is quite easy. Once you have selected a CD, you can type in search words (key words), or you can select words from a menu or list offered by the database. The computer searches the database for information on the subjects you have selected and reports the number of entries on those subjects that it has found in the database. You can then look at a list of entries and choose to view the long display on any of them. On some databases, the display will show bibliographic information only; on other databases, the display will include the full text of an article.

CD-ROMs are produced by several database companies, and the search process may differ slightly depending on the company whose CD-ROMs you are using. Different databases also emphasize different sorts of information. In general, on any database, you should be able to access both indexes and the full text of magazines, journals, newspapers, and other publications, which are often arranged by professional sphere (e.g., academic publications) or by general subject matter (e.g., the *Biological and Agricultural Index,* available from H. W. Wilson).

RESEARCH 7

TAKING NOTES BASED ON YOUR RESEARCH

Once you are equipped with a focused question and know how to find the information that will help you answer that question, you are ready to take notes.

Taking good notes will urge you to read more carefully; conversely, reading carefully will help you to take good notes. You have already learned some reading strategies for doing efficient and thorough research. Taking notes involves selecting and synthesizing the most important information from your sources. Note-taking will help you to develop ideas and arguments and to gain a thorough knowledge of your topic.

You can respond to the sources you consult in many ways; in this section, you will learn ways to:

- copy factual information
- copy quotations
- paraphrase
- summarize
- ask questions
- follow up ideas with research

Observations, ideas, and questions will occur to you while you read and consider sources. These responses represent your own perspective and creativity; they will help you to write an interesting and coherent paper. Some students jot down key words and generalities that later will suggest directions to pursue and connections to make. Others take a break from note-taking to follow through fully on a thought.

One student, for example, was doing research for her paper on architectural restoration in historic but low-rent neighborhoods in Chicago. She came across a newspaper article on rent-districting policies, which reminded her of a book she had read on residential overcrowding in urban areas. She stopped reading the article to list the possible ways in which architectural restoration in some neighborhoods might produce overcrowding in others by influencing rents. She later used this list to develop the thesis of her paper. Another student may have made a brief note of the relationship between restoration and overcrowding and waited until he got home to think more about it. If you are reading carefully, you may find it useful to analyze and interpret the source at that moment; if you are skimming, you may want simply to note digressive responses briefly and reserve more thoughtful work for later.

In the beginning stages of your research, it may be difficult to tell which information is worth noting. It is better, in this case, to take more notes than fewer: Even seemingly irrelevant information may become quite useful to you at a later stage in your thinking. It is not a waste of time to write down more information than you will use in your paper; thorough note-taking will give you the flexibility to choose the best evidence for your paper.

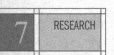

Using Quotations

Direct quotations are the easiest notes to take and document. Although you may write down many quotations in the course of research, remember that quotations are *evidence* for your own assertions or analysis. Quotations cannot substitute for your own analysis; rather, they can be used to support your analysis. When you read and take notes, try to limit the number of direct quotations you list. Look for particularly pertinent passages: those that speak most strongly and directly to your point and those that are well phrased (clear, specific, descriptive). These passages are the best candidates for quotations. Quotations are also valuable when they derive from people who are well known or who are strong, respected authorities—in other words, from authors whose opinions are important.

You can test the quotability of a text by trying to paraphrase or summarize it. If you can't do either—if it simply doesn't make sense to put the passage into other words—but the content of the text is still important, then you should quote it. For example, Alex, a student who is writing a 20-page research paper on modern travel writing, is in the process of reading some travel narratives. One of these, Paul Theroux's *The Pillars of Hercules: A Grand Tour of the Mediterranean,* opens with a line that really appeals to Alex:

> People here in Western Civilization say that tourists are no different from apes, but on the Rock of Gibraltar, one of the Pillars of Hercules, I saw both tourists and apes together, and I learned to tell them apart (1).

Alex can use this sentence in his paper to demonstrate Theroux's style, perspective, and intentions, but to do this, he must use Theroux's exact words. The sentence will not be valuable if it is rephrased.

If you wish to quote a passage of a text but don't need each and every word in that passage, you can use ellipses to show your interruption of the original text. In the following passage from Theroux's book, Alex notices something he thinks is characteristic of modern travel writing:

> We soon came to a checkpoint, with Bosnian soldiers, and some policemen who entered the bus and bullied civilians, denouncing them for carrying doubtful-looking identity papers. There were Croatian checkpoints, too, at Omis, Makarska, and Podgorje: the same routine. Usually the victim of the policeman's wrath was a squirming, cowering woman. In this sort of situation the cop had absolute power: he could arrest the poor woman or boot her off the bus, or send her back where she came from (241).

Alex decides that he doesn't need to quote the entire passage. Instead, he transcribes only the most relevant part of the passage and inserts ellipses (three dots) to signal the part of the text he has left out:

> We soon came to the checkpoint, with Bosnian soldiers, and some policemen who entered the bus and bullied civilians. . . . Usually the victim of the policeman's wrath was a squirming, cowering woman. In this sort of situation the cop had absolute power . . . (241).

The part that Alex quoted is the part he needed to make his point.

Once Alex identified the passage he wanted to include in his own paper, he knew he needed to introduce the passage so the reader would know who contributed it. Here's how Alex accomplished integrating the quotation into his own paper:

> As Theroux described his trip to Bosnia, readers can feel the daily tension. "We soon came to a checkpoint, with Bosnian soldiers, and some policemen who entered the bus and bullied civilians," Theroux reported. "Usually the victim of the policeman's wrath was a squirming, cowering woman" (241).

Paraphrasing

Paraphrasing is tricky because it is the form of note-taking that lends itself most easily to plagiarism. It is useful to think of paraphrases as reports: For instance, when you "report" an opinion you heard on the radio about the new Congressional tax policy, you are uninvolved in the opinion—your interpretation is not required—but when you report the opinion, you do so in your own way, in your own language. You should paraphrase when you don't want to quote directly, either because it is not called for (for the reasons listed above) or because the language is difficult (overly scientific, full of jargon, etc.), yet most of the content of the paraphrased material is needed.

The important thing to remember in paraphrasing is that you want your paraphrase to resemble the original passage only in its main points—not in length, style, or structure. The first step in paraphrasing a passage of a text is to read it through. Once you understand the content of the passage, you can select its important points—those key to the author's argument (*not* necessarily key to yours). You may rearrange these points in the order that makes the most sense to you: You have the opportunity here to edit and clarify the author's writing. Finally, you are ready to restate the author's points in your own words. Here, you should not simply "translate" an author's sentences into very similar sentences of your own, which differ only in vocabulary. Rather, you should try to write the paraphrase in your own style. It will be easier to know your own style once you start writing your paper; at that stage, you may wish to change the paraphrasing you have done in your notes.

Paraphrased sources need to be documented by a footnote, endnote, or parenthetical citation, just as you would do with a quotation. It also helps the reader if you introduce a paraphrased source by referring to the author or the source in your own sentence. You want the reader to know that this passage of your writing really has a basis in someone else's work.

Alex has read several primary sources for his paper, and he is now consulting secondary sources as well. One of his secondary sources is an article by Adrian Furnham called "Tourism and Culture Shock," in which Furnham offers his own interpretation of travel. Alex finds one of Furnham's observations particularly striking:

Anyone who lives in a popular tourist city or town soon becomes aware of the fact that it is not only the tourists who experience culture shock at the behavior and beliefs of natives, but also the natives who experience culture shock at the unusual habits of tourists (53).

Although this sentence contains an important insight, it is somewhat unwieldy, and the writing style is not appealing to Alex. He decides to paraphrase the sentence. When he discusses Furnham in his paper, Alex writes:

Adrian Furnham shows us the flip side of the conventional travel perspective in his article "Tourism and Culture Shock." After reviewing the psychological literature on the effects of travel on tourists, he considers the experience of people who are subjected to tourism (Furnham 1984: 53). Furnham argues that people who live in tourist areas experience the same kind of "culture shock" that tourists do: Tourists and "natives" are equally strange to one another.

Here, Alex effectively combines a paraphrase with direct quotations of key words—"culture shock" and "natives"—from Furnham's article. He selects what is most important from Furnham's text and restates it in his own writing style, which is easily distinguished from Furnham's.

Summarizing

In comparison with using quotations and paraphrasing, summarizing involves more reading and less writing. Summarizing requires that you understand the main points of a passage and not be distracted by details that the author includes to support those points. A summary consists mainly of generalizations.

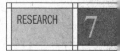

RESEARCH   7

You can usually judge whether to summarize a passage rather than paraphrase it on the basis of its length. You wouldn't want to paraphrase a 30-page chapter of a book, but you can easily summarize it.

In summarizing, as in paraphrasing, you should read a text thoroughly and to the end. While you read, look in paragraphs or groups of paragraphs for topic sentences. These are sentences that state a section's main point, for which the rest of the information is supporting argument or detail; they are the sentences you might underline or highlight if you were reading your own copy of the work. In some sources you consult, you will not find clear topic sentences. In this case, you will need to gather parts of the author's main points from a number of sentences.

When you have finished reading, use the main ideas you have identified in topic or other sentences to write your summary. You should write these main points in your own language and in the order that makes the most sense to you. Because you will be omitting many of the author's finer points, your summary should represent a different arrangement of ideas from the original.

DOCUMENTING SOURCES

When you take notes, you will need to record complete information about every source you consult. However, you may not want to rewrite all of this information for each piece of information you jot down. It may be easiest to transcribe full bibliographic information from your sources onto a master list of sources, to which you can add in the course of your research. You can then refer to these sources in abbreviated form in your notes.

In your master list, you should record the following information:

- author(s) and/or editor(s)
- complete title
- city of publication
- publisher
- edition
- year of publication (if the source is a reprint or numbered edition, you'll need the original and the most recent copyright dates)
- volume (with scholarly journal articles, you may need to note volume and number, e.g., vol. 3, no. 1)
- page numbers (for a section of a book, a journal, or a newspaper article)

When you are ready to compile a bibliography of works you have consulted in your research or cited in your paper, this master list will be invaluable.

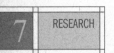

There are several acceptable ways to document your sources; you should ask your instructor which style is appropriate for your paper. To start, you should know the difference between bibliographic entries and footnotes or endnotes. Your bibliography is a list, arranged alphabetically by author's last name, of all the works you cited or consulted. The bibliography typically does not provide page numbers for material taken from books. For instance, Clara wrote a paper on the dramatic uses of heat in a novel by Doris Lessing. Her bibliographic entry for the novel looked like this:

Lessing, Doris. *The Grass Is Singing*. New York: Plume, [1950] 1978.

Note that the entry is not indented. If an entry requires more than one line, all lines after the first line should be indented five spaces. You should double-space bibliographic entries and skip two double-spaced lines between entries.

Footnotes and endnotes are the actual citations of sources: You use them to provide information about the sources you quote, paraphrase, summarize, or otherwise reference in your paper. Footnotes and endnotes are numbered consecutively to match the superscript number in the text of your paper. Footnotes appear at the bottom of the page of your paper where the cited material appears; endnotes appear in a list at the end of your paper. In addition to source information, you can also provide additional facts or commentary in a footnote or endnote. Clara quoted Lessing's novel in the following section in her paper:

> Mary's increasing anxiety both flows from and exacerbates the intense South African heat: "And it really seemed to her that she could not stand another morning with the hot sun on her neck, with the dazzle of heat in her eyes, although she felt sick with the heat when she stayed in the house. . . . As time passed, the heat became an obsession."[3]

Clara's corresponding note at the foot of the page (or in a list at the end of the paper) looked like this:

> [3]Doris Lessing, *The Grass Is Singing* (New York: Plume, [1950] 1978) 75. Such descriptions of the heat recur throughout Lessing's book—one reason it is known for its vivid realism.

Notice that, among other differences between the note citation and the bibliographic entry, the note's first line is indented and the subsequent lines are not.

If you use full footnotes or endnotes such as Clara's, you may not need to attach a separate bibliography at the end of your paper because all the information that would appear in a bibliographic entry will appear in your notes instead. You should provide all of this information for a source only the first time you cite that source. Thereafter, you can use the short form: Simply include the author's last name, the year of publication if you use more than one source from that author, and the page number where the cited material appears.

Another option is to use only the short form for all of your footnotes or endnotes. In this case, you will need to attach a bibliography or list of works cited.

Another way to document sources is to use parenthetical citations, which are internal or textual notes. These notes include abbreviated source information and appear in parentheses in the text of your paper. If you use internal notes, you must provide a full bibliography or list of works cited. You can then refer to the bibliography in your notes.

If Clara had used parenthetical citation, she would have written:

> Mary's increasing anxiety both flows from and exacerbates the intense South African heat: "And it really seemed to her that she could not stand another morning with the hot sun on her neck, with the dazzle of heat in her eyes, although she felt sick with the heat when she stayed in the house. . . . As time passed, the heat became an obsession" (Lessing 1978: 75).

This parenthetical note includes the author's name, the year of the work's publication, and the page number where the quoted material appears. This information leads the reader to the source in the bibliography.

Styles of Documentation

Well-known manuals for documentation style include the *MLA Handbook for Writers of Research Papers,* which is the standard style for humanities papers, and the American Psychological Association's *Publication Manual,* which is the standard for social science papers.

MLA style of documentation. Although your professor may ask you to use footnotes or endnotes, preferred MLA style cites sources within parentheses. After quotations or paraphrased material, indicate the author and page number of the cited work, the way Clara did when citing Lessing, in the example above. The citation is then expanded fully in a list of works cited. Here are examples of bibliographic entries in MLA style:

> Furnham, Adrian. "Tourism and Culture Shock." *Annals of Tourism Research*, Vol. 11. 1984: 41–57.
> Theroux, Paul. *The Pillars of Hercules: A Grand Tour of the Mediterranean*. New York: G.P. Putnam's Sons, 1995.
> Wonter, Janine. "Tourism Totters in the Mediterranean." *The Granham Flier*. 31 Aug. 1994: 67–68.

APA style of documentation. In the social sciences, the date of publication often is crucial in evaluating a source's significance. Therefore, you'll notice that the date of publication comes earlier in the citation in the APA style than in the MLA style. If you use the APA style, you will cite sources not with footnotes or endnotes, but with internal (parenthetical) notes. You will attach a list of works cited in the bibliographic form that you see in the examples below:

> Furnham, A. (1984). Tourism and culture shock. *Annals of Tourism Research, 11*, 41–57.
> Theroux, P. (1995). *The pillars of Hercules: A grand tour of the Mediterranean*. New York: G.P. Putnam's Sons.
> Wonter, J. (1994, Aug. 31). Tourism totters in the Mediterranean. *The Granham Flier*, pp. 67–68.

Online sources may offer standard bibliographic information. For instance, if you read an article from *The New York Times* on the Internet—either at the newspaper's official Web site or posted by an individual at a different site—you should document it as if you were reading it in hard copy. Other online sources may not include such information. In this case, record the date on which you read the information, the electronic source (Internet address, database), and the author or sender of the information.

ORGANIZING YOUR NOTES

The method you use to organize your notes may depend on your experience, library facilities, and advice of classmates and instructors. Whether you use note cards, a notebook, or a computer, you should make sure to identify the source of each note on the note itself. Head each set of notes with a source reference, a subject or key word, and the page numbers concerned. For direct quotes, the page numbers you list should be only those pages on which quoted words appear; for paraphrases and summaries, list the numbers of all the pages from which you draw information.

When you take notes, make sure to keep your personal responses separate from quotations, paraphrases, and summaries. If you write responses and notes in the same place—on the same note card, sheet of paper, or computer file—you can distinguish your responses by bracketing them or putting headings on them. However, it may be safer to write responses and notes on separate note cards, on the front and back of the same cards, on different pages or sections in a notebook, or in different files on a computer (you can keep both windows open at once).

Index Cards

Index cards impose great discipline. This form of note-taking is sometimes arduous and cumbersome, but it will improve your organizational skills.

Index cards make it easy for you to keep brief notes—whose content can fit on a card or two—and to keep notes on different topics in different places. Often, using different-colored cards for different subject areas helps you to keep the cards organized. They also allow you to cross-index your notes. For instance, if you have copied down part of a senator's speech that covers crime rates and employment statistics, you can keep two different note cards in two separate files: one on crime and one on employment. Cross-indexing will let you remember what notes you have and therefore help you make the most efficient use of them.

RESEARCH 7

If you take notes on index cards, keep separate cards for different sources, different quotes, distinct points, and so forth. To organize these cards, try writing a subject heading on each one. Later, when you are ready to start writing your outline and your paper, you can spread all of your cards out (on a table or the floor) and see them all at once. You can then try different ways of arranging the information you have collected. In addition, the extra step of filing your note cards will permit you to estimate how much information you have on each point for your paper; it will also remind you of what notes you've already taken so that you don't duplicate your efforts.

Index cards have some disadvantages. For one thing, they are easy to lose. For another, they are quite small and will not allow you to take long, substantive notes easily. You can, of course, take one set of notes on multiple index cards. If you do this, you will need to attach cards with a continuing note together or make sure to rewrite the same heading on each one. Otherwise, you risk losing the source for a set of notes, which means you will have to go back to the library to find it.

Notebooks

Notebooks offer more room and flexibility than index cards. Notebooks are preferable if you like to read hard copy rather than computer screens and if you think best while writing as opposed to typing. If you do use a notebook, make sure that you invent an indexing system: You can organize notes into sections by subject, source, or some other meaningful feature.

One disadvantage of using a notebook is the inability to spread out your notes and look at many at once: You can see only what is on one page.

Tape Recorders

Especially if you are an auditory learner, the tape recorder may be a useful tool for recording notes. Some students find that they can work more quickly if they read into a tape recorder rather than copy material from sources. At the same time, reading aloud helps them to process the material.

Computer Files

Computers have a much larger—nearly infinite—capacity for storing information; if you are planning a massive amount of research, they are your best bet. Computers also permit continual reorganization: If you take notes on a computer, you will be able to make corrections and additions easily, without disrupting the order of your notes. Another advantage of note-taking by computer is that when you get to writing your paper, you can transfer notes directly from a note file into your paper's file: You won't have to rewrite everything (as you do if you take notes on paper). If you prefer to read and work from hard copy rather than from a computer screen, you can always print your notes before starting to write your paper.

With most word processing software, you can keep several note files open at once and simply shift between windows. This capability will be quite helpful if you find that a source is useful on several subjects, or if you are keeping separate files for your personal responses and your notes. You can organize these note files into folders by subject, source, or whatever organizational scheme you prefer. This way, as you take more notes and add files for them, you will have to choose a research category for each new note. This will help you to stay on target and avoid distractions in your research.

PLAGIARISM AND OVERDOCUMENTATION

Although it should now be clear to you *how* to document a source, you may still have questions about *when* you should do it. This section will help you make good decisions about citing the information you use, directly or indirectly, in your paper. You must document a source if you use quoted, paraphrased, or summarized material. You should cite other people's original insights, observations, and arguments, as well as their data, figures, and research results. Take particular care to document information your readers may want to look at for themselves in the original source, either because it is surprising or because the source contains additional useful information.

On the other hand, you do not have to document everything you learn from your research. You do not have to document information that most readers may know and statements they would generally accept, for example, general facts about major historical events (the French Revolution started in 1789); the names and roles of public and mythic figures (the British Prime Minister Tony Blair was elected in 1997); or even more specific information that is both indisputable and widely available. Likewise, elementary scientific facts and explanations (heat rises, meat is a source of protein), general observations (commuters read newspapers), and other sorts of common "truths" are the property of everyone, including you. Of course, your own ideas, arguments, and analyses do not need to be documented.

What Is Plagiarism?

RESEARCH   7

Students sometimes encounter cases in which the basic, commonsense documentation guidelines do not seem to apply. When you do the sorts of research we've discussed in this chapter, it will often be clear which evidence you should cite in your paper. For instance, Joe was writing a paper on lung cancer rates in American cities. He knew that he had to cite the useful figures he found in an article by Dr. Lamm, an urban oncologist. He also knew that he should cite Dr. Lamm's analysis of the figures because it supported Joe's own argument. However, it was less clear to Joe *how* he ought to cite this evidence, especially since he was having trouble distinguishing his thoughts from Dr. Lamm's.

This is the kind of situation in which plagiarism can occur. Plagiarism is a term most people recognize but don't clearly understand. Because plagiarism is a serious legal and moral issue with significant consequences for your career as a student, it is important for you to have an adequate grasp of what it means.

Broadly speaking, **plagiarism** means that you take credit—either deliberately or by accident—for observations, ideas, arguments, phrases, and figures that you gather in the course of your research. There are obvious and subtle forms of plagiarism: A direct quotation that appears in a student's paper without quotation marks is a fairly clear case; an idea that is partly the student's but partly a well-known essayist's is less apparent—but still plagiarism. Recall the passage from Adrian Furnham's article that Alex used in his paper on travel writing:

> Anyone who lives in a popular tourist city or town soon becomes aware of the fact that it is not only the tourists who experience culture shock at the behavior and beliefs of natives, but also the natives who experience culture shock at the unusual habits of tourists (Furnham 1984: 53).

Earlier, in the section on taking notes, you saw how Alex used an acceptable paraphrase of this sentence. A different student poorly paraphrased the same sentence and did not cite Furnham at all:

> Tourists are not the only ones who get culture shock. People who live in places that tourists visit are "shocked" by the "culture" of the tourists, too.

Here, Furnham's idea is merely rephrased; even the order in which his ideas are arranged is conserved. Without a citation, this paraphrase is plagiarism.

Equally bad is the following version, in which another student copied portions from the original text directly:

> It is a fact that the natives of popular tourist cities experience culture shock. The behavior and beliefs of tourists are as disturbing to natives as natives are to tourists.

Another student, who was interested in finding support for his own disapproval of tourists, engaged in a more complex form of plagiarism in this paragraph:

> Tourists are not at all sensitive to the natives of the regions they visit. Tourists experience "culture shock" when they meet these people, who are very different from them in their customs, appearance, and perspective. Natives, although they also may experience culture shock when faced with the rude behavior of tourists, are less blameworthy: They did not ask for their shocking experience, whereas the tourists are the sole cause of their own discomfort (Furnham 1984: 53).

This version is an interpretation, not a representation, of Furnham. Furnham is cited, but it is not at all clear which of the ideas expressed belong to Furnham, and it looks as if Furnham is credited with ideas and opinions that we know do not appear in the original article. As this example shows, documentation must be specific.

When Does Plagiarism Occur?

Plagiarism does not have to be intentional. In fact, most often, it is a consequence of hurried work. If you do not have adequate time to take notes—which means not only writing complete bibliographic information for each source you consult, but also reading each source carefully and thinking about how it may be useful to you—you may find yourself either short of ideas or full of ideas that aren't yours. Also, people make poor decisions when they are tired or under stress—feelings familiar to many students. To avoid plagiarism, it is best to be prepared with good notes and a firm grasp of your own ideas *before* you start to write, so you don't have to rely solely on your state of mind.

Sometimes, students plagiarize because they don't quite know how to use their sources properly. Particularly with a research paper, you may feel unequipped to judge the evidence you are required to use as support for your argument. You may feel overwhelmed by the volume of expert opinions published by professional critics, essayists, and scientists. You might think you have nothing additional to say, or perhaps you don't feel qualified to dispute anyone else. These experiences are common for students who rely too heavily on others' opinions—that is, on secondary sources—rather than concentrating on the primary sources about which they need to develop their own opinions.

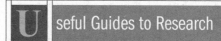

U | seful Guides to Research

The following guides may help you with general and specific research concerns:

Berkman, Robert I. *Find It Fast: How to Uncover Expert Information on Any Subject, In Print or Online*. New York: Harper Perennial, 1997 (including a particularly detailed section on the Internet, in addition to full information on library resources).

Booth, Wayne C., Gregory G. Colomb, and Joseph Williams. *The Craft of Research*. Chicago: University of Chicago Press, 1995 (helpful for devising topics and questions, and for weighing and using evidence).

Johnson, Jean. *The Bedford Guide to the Research Process*. Boston: Bedford Books, 1992 (especially strong on advice for note-taking).

RESEARCH 7

How Can You Avoid Plagiarism?

The best strategy for avoiding plagiarism is to use the note-taking methods of quotation, paraphrasing, and summary, as described above, as a model in your writing. The rules you follow in taking notes are the same rules you should follow in writing; if you do not plagiarize in your notes, you are unlikely to do so in your writing. You should attribute every quote, every paraphrase, and every summary to a source. You also should write good paraphrases and summaries—ones that capture the essential points in an author's argument but that are written in your own style.

Note-taking will help you avoid plagiarism in another way. In taking good notes, you are taking the time to read your sources carefully, to think about them, and to identify which parts of which sources you will use for which purposes. Your notes are your written records of these processes; they will make it much easier for you to remember where the line is between your ideas and those of other people. If you are not careful taking notes (simply copying sentences without thinking about how they fit into your own ideas and plans for your paper), you may not even realize, later on, that an idea that has "just occurred" to you actually came from someone else.

When you incorporate sources into your paper, signal the origins of those sources: "Dr. Ann Kaliphos, in her new book *The Vegetarian Life,* suggests that the principal health benefit of abstaining from meat is an increased vitamin intake." You may flag your own ideas with the first-person voice: "I, on the other hand, will argue that the true vegetarian success is a moralistic one." You should be careful to take credit for your own ideas, not bury them in a summary or paraphrase of someone else's point of view.

Are You Overdocumenting?

People who are anxious about plagiarism sometimes overcompensate by citing each and every idea expressed in their papers. If you are in doubt about whether to cite a piece of evidence, you should err on the side of caution. But if you find that you are documenting almost every sentence, you may be writing nothing more than a report of other people's ideas. You need to do the work of interpreting, analyzing, and responding to the evidence you find.

Research is an essential part of academic work, and it can be fulfilling and productive once you learn the strategies discussed in this chapter. Once you have done your research, read your sources, and taken notes, you will be ready to begin the next step: writing a college paper. Chapter 8 offers help on the writing process.

7 | RESEARCH

ADDITIONAL RESOURCES

Buckley, Peter and Duncan Clark. *The Rough Guide to the Internet.* London: Rough Guides, 2007.

Gibaldi, Joseph. *MLA Handbook for Writers of Research Papers,* 6th ed. New York: Modern Language Association, 2003.

Leshin, Cynthia B. *Student Resource Guide to the Internet: Student Success Online.* Upper Saddle River, NJ: Prentice Hall, 1998.

Publication Manual of the American Psychological Association, 5th ed. Washington, D.C.: American Psychological Association, 2001.

Sometimes I sit at the computer and nothing happens. Nothing. The blank screen just stares back at me, and the longer I sit the worse it gets. It's like a face-off at the OK Corral, and eventually the computer wins.

Jon Everett,
student

STRATEGIES FOR WRITING

Every writer—at one time or another—has sat in front of a computer screen or typewriter keyboard with nothing to say and a deadline to meet. Contrary to popular myth, however, writer's block is not an incurable disease. It usually is caused by a problem at one stage of the writing process—a process that begins much earlier than the moment you sit down in front of the ominous blank screen. Writing a successful paper starts when you get your assignment and ends when you complete the final revision of your work.

In this chapter, you'll learn how to:

- understand your assignment
- generate and develop ideas
- draft an essay
- revise globally and locally.

WRITER'S BLOCK: WHAT IS IT AND WHAT CAUSES IT?

The chilling experience that some writers call **writer's block** is an inability to generate ideas. Usually, that feeling of powerlessness and despair has one of five causes.

1. *You don't understand the assignment.* Suppose someone led you into a workshop where you found planks of wood, a can of nails, a saw, and a hammer, and that person told you you'd be paid when the job was done. Certainly you'd want to know exactly what you were expected to build, for example, a

Writing Assignment Checklist

Here are some questions to ask yourself about any writing assignment:

1. Is this assignment testing my knowledge of class lectures and readings, or is it asking me to go beyond that material?
2. Am I required to use outside sources? If so, what sources are appropriate?
3. Is the thesis or argument given to me by the assignment, or do I have to invent my own?
4. Am I focusing on one text or comparing one text with another?
5. Do I need to define key terms?
6. If I am analyzing a text, does the assignment ask me to consider any of the following?

   - the author's background or life
   - the author's motivation for writing the text
   - the historical or cultural context of the text
   - the original audience for the text
   - the writing strategies used by the author
   - the main themes of the text
   - the form or structure of the text
   - the emotional or intellectual effect the text has on me

---

8 WRITING

desk or a dog house. The more information you had, the more likely it would be that you'd build something pleasing to your employer. Without that information, you'd probably develop a case of builder's block.

Any writing assignment should clearly explain your task as a writer, tell you what sources you should use, indicate how long the paper should be, and give you a due date. When you get a writing assignment from your instructor, make sure you understand what you are asked to do. If you feel confused or unsure, *ask your instructor* as soon as possible. Don't wait until the day before the assignment is due.

2. *You haven't done the required reading for the class.* If you haven't kept up with reading assignments, you'll have trouble with writing assignments. Even when you tackle assignments that require additional research beyond class readings, your instructor will expect that you have listened to lectures, participated in class discussions, and done all the required work. Sometimes, falling behind in your class work—and therefore developing writer's block—is a

result of poor time management. See Chapter 4 for help with time management strategies.

3. *You haven't done preliminary writing.* Any athlete will tell you that if you try to run, swim, ski, lift weights, or do anything physically demanding without warming up, you won't perform well. It's the same with writing. Before you sit down to begin your paper, there are some strategies that can help you to "warm up" and generate ideas. In the next section of this chapter, you'll learn some of those strategies.

4. *You're afraid of being judged.* "I have quite a bit of difficulty separating the product from the person," Patricia Adams admits. "When I write, I feel as though I am taking a piece of myself, a very private and intimate piece, and putting it on paper to be judged by anyone who can read." Your instructor, who will give you a grade on your work, does take on the role of judge. But more important, she is interested in helping you develop your ideas. Writing serves as an important way of communicating those ideas.

If fear of being judged is getting in the way of your writing, make an appointment to see your instructor to discuss the problem. You'll find that your instructor's understanding and sympathy will go a long way toward easing your fears. Many instructors will look at early drafts or passages from your paper and offer suggestions for revision or simply let you know that you're on the right track. Communicating with your instructor as early as possible in the writing process may give you the support you need to overcome writer's block.

5. *You didn't leave enough time.* Writing takes time. Even if you have done all your reading, research, preliminary writing, and outlining, you can count on producing about four or five pages of writing in a few hours of work. If you have to produce a ten-page paper, you may need two four-hour sessions of writing to complete a first draft and, a day or two later, another few hours for revision. If you sit down in front of your computer or typewriter the night before a paper is due, your anxiety about time may well result in writer's block. Chapter 4 gives you some hints on organizing your time when you have to complete a writing project.

WRITING   8

GENERATING IDEAS

No one can write a good paper without good ideas. How do you come up with those ideas? By thinking, recording your ideas, reflecting on those ideas, and thinking some more.

Good ideas come from good questions. Sometimes your instructor will provide you with a question to address in your paper. Often, though, it is your responsibility to come up with a question of your own. In Chapter 7, you learned some strategies for formulating questions based on your interest in a certain topic. A good question for a college essay:

- asks you to make an argument or analysis
- cannot be answered by a simple yes or no
- is focused enough so that it can be answered in a college-length essay
- genuinely interests you and therefore is likely to interest your readers

Here are a few examples of questions that could result in good college papers:

Course:	*Nineteenth-Century American History*
Topic:	Theodore Roosevelt
Question:	How did Theodore Roosevelt's relationship with his sons reflect his ideas about manhood?
Sources:	Roosevelt's letters to his children

Course:	*Health Services and the Law*
Topic:	Nursing home regulation
Question:	What can Florida's regulatory measures teach legislators about state intervention in nursing homes?
Sources:	*Miami Herald* articles, Florida statutes on nursing home care, interviews with nursing home administrators

Course:	*Economics of International Business*
Topic:	Marketing American products in Asia
Question:	Coca-Cola has shaped its marketing strategy to respond to national tastes in Thailand, Cambodia, and Viet Nam. Where has the company's strategy proved most successful? Why?
Sources:	*Wall Street Journal* articles, *Business Week* articles, Internet sources, Coca-Cola annual reports

In the examples above, these questions are specific enough to discuss in a college essay. The sources that will help a student to answer the questions are all primary sources.

So how do you get started? Most students find that ideas will flow if they sit down and write in a journal or notebook, on index cards, or on their computer. Without worrying about the final product, without the pressure of organizing their thoughts, they find that freewriting exercises, in whatever form, help them to think creatively.

Journal Writing

A journal can take many forms: a computer file in which you make a daily entry, a notebook in which you jot down ideas as they occur to you, or even a tape recorder, into which you can talk as you commute to or from work. Busy students find that making a record of ideas helps to jump-start the writing and research process.

Freewriting, Brainstorming, and Mind-Mapping

When you freewrite, brainstorm, or mind-map, you write down any idea, in any order, without worrying about making logical connections. Freewriting can take many forms, including lists, sentences, phrases, and diagrams. Freewriting lets you generate an abundance of material, which you can edit and shape when you sit down to write your first draft. When you see your ideas on paper, you can connect them with arrows to come up with a "map" of ideas that can lead you to a useful outline. See the following illustration for an example of freewriting.

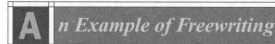

An Example of Freewriting

"Theodore Roosevelt's Ideas on Manhood"

Consider the illustrated example that follows. A student began freewriting by jotting down the title of Theodore Roosevelt's famous essay on manhood, "The Strenuous Life." Then, using arrows, the student noted which aspects of life Roosevelt himself thought were strenuous, that is, war, exercise, hunting, and risk-taking. Beginning with these words, the student then wrote down other associated words that popped into his head. As he looked at these words, the student discovered that the word *power* was important in all the areas Roosevelt wrote about. By linking this recurring word, the student began to see a pattern in Roosevelt's thinking. This pattern helped the student make his own analysis of what the "strenuous life" and manhood meant to Theodore Roosevelt.

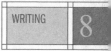

WRITING

8

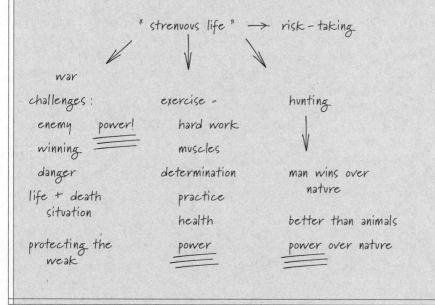

Starting with Passages from Source Material

Often, typing out passages from a text helps you to analyze them. Typing forces you to think about the passage slowly and to "process" it more thoroughly than if you only underlined or highlighted it.

Outlining

It's likely that all of us learned how to make an outline at some time in our school careers. With Roman numerals, letters, and Arabic numbers, we organized our ideas into a plan that was supposed to structure our paper. Some of us, however, became proficient outliners without being able to transfer the outline structure to our actual writing.

More detailed—and potentially more helpful—than such an outline, a paragraph outline gives you a chance to think through an organizational plan for your paper, build in transitions, and begin to develop your ideas. A **paragraph outline** contains the main idea for each section of your paper and includes several sentences explaining that idea and showing ways that you can support it. A paragraph outline is useful to help organize the ideas generated by some form of freewriting.

S ample Paragraph Outline

How did Theodore Roosevelt's relationship with his sons reflect his ideas about manhood?

I. Introduction. Brief overview of Roosevelt's life. In this section, I'll tell about his marriage and give dates for the birth of his sons.

II. Roosevelt's ideas about manhood. In this paragraph, I'll talk about "The Strenuous Life," the essay where Roosevelt talks about a man's responsibilities and how men should behave.

III. Kermit. In this paragraph, I'll describe Kermit and tell what kind of a boy he was. Source will be biographies of Roosevelt.

IV. Relationship between Kermit and his father. I'll use letters from Roosevelt to Kermit about athletics at Harvard to show what Roosevelt valued.

V. Quentin. In this paragraph, I'll describe Quentin and tell what kind of boy he was. Source will be biographies of Roosevelt.

VI. Relationship with Quentin. What activities did Roosevelt share with his son?

VII. Conclusion. I'll relate my findings to the ideas that Roosevelt discussed in "The Strenuous Life" to show how the essay can be seen as an explanation of his relationship with his sons.

Visualizing a Reader

As you write, explain your ideas to a specific person. Your "imaginary reader" might be unknown to you or might be an interested friend, a sympathetic instructor, or a classmate who shares your interests.

PLANNING

Your plan need not be a formal outline with each section and subsection numbered. Some students use images and shapes to help them visualize the paper's organization. Some students create a map, moving from one point to another as they create a "road" of ideas.

Having a plan, however, will help you as you draft your paper. Here are five questions to keep in mind as you construct your plan:

1. What information does your reader need as background?

2. What are the main points you want to make in the essay?

3. How will you construct a transition between one point and the next?

4. Where will you include your evidence?

5. What might someone with an opposing view argue? Where will you consider opposing views in the paper?

DRAFTING

Any piece of college writing contains a beginning, where the reader discovers the focus of the paper; a middle section, where assertions are presented, supported by evidence; and a conclusion. These sections vary in length, depending on the length of the total paper. A two-page essay may well fit into the famous five-paragraph model: one paragraph for an introduction, three paragraphs for development, one paragraph for a conclusion.

WRITING 8

In a five- to seven-page paper, which is a popular length for college essays, the introduction may consist of several paragraphs, the development may cover several pages, and the conclusion may take one or more paragraphs.

Writing an Introduction

The first paragraphs of an essay should tell the reader, clearly and precisely, what the paper is about. Your reader should discover what question you are asking, what argument or analysis you are making in response to that question, and what sources you are using to answer the question.

A strong first paragraph also will help your reader understand the context for your question and, therefore, your paper. For example, the student writing about Theodore Roosevelt's relationship with his sons was interested in Roosevelt's self-proclaimed courage and manliness. The student learned from the course that Roosevelt's phrase "the strenuous life" served to defend many aspects of American culture, from international politics to the building of the Panama Canal. *In that context,* looking at how Roosevelt communicated his values to his children seemed interesting. A strong introduction would present this context so that the reader understands why the student is interested in answering the question about Roosevelt's relationship with his sons.

Weak introductions are vague and unfocused, such as this one for a literature paper:

> Kate Chopin's *The Awakening* can be looked at from many points of view. Many critics have examined the novel to see what it tells us about Chopin's ideas about women's lives. Indeed, by looking at the women artists in the novel, they discover some interesting things.

Except for finding out that this person will be writing on Kate Chopin's *The Awakening,* the reader will have no idea what "interesting things" critics have said about Chopin's women artists. Most important, the reader doesn't know what the writer thinks. In college, you are asked to do more than report about what other people think; you need to come up with an idea of your own.

Here is a better introduction on the same topic:

> Kate Chopin's *The Awakening* shows us the conflicts some women face when they want to express their creativity. When we look at the lives of two women artists in the novel, we can see that Chopin took a pessimistic view of the possibility of being a wife, mother, and artist.

This introduction tells the reader specifically the question being asked: What does Chopin think about the possibility of a woman's being a wife, mother, and artist? It tells the reader that in this paper, the writer both looks at two women artists and thinks Chopin's view is pessimistic. This writer has done a good job in just two sentences.

Your introduction may be one paragraph in a fairly short essay or several paragraphs in a longer essay. Some useful strategies for introductions include:

- beginning with a question
- beginning with a quotation
- beginning with an anecdote or illustration

Developing Paragraphs

A paragraph consists of a group of sentences that develops and supports an assertion. Usually, that assertion is expressed in the topic sentence. The topic sentence helps the reader to anticipate what idea you will develop in the paragraph. The rest of the paragraph develops the idea by offering evidence and supporting details. Each sentence in the paragraph relates to the main idea.

In papers that are longer than a page or two, you often cannot develop ideas fully in one paragraph. In that case, you will create paragraph **clusters** of two, three, or four paragraphs. Each paragraph within that cluster develops a subtopic of the main idea.

Within a paragraph, sentences follow one another logically. Sentences can be connected by **transitions** or by **repetition** of words. Here is one paragraph that uses both strategies:

> The controversy over home schooling focuses on the need for students to become socialized through **interaction** with other students. That **interaction,** in class and through extracurricular activities, helps students learn how to share ideas, work on teams, and respect others' needs. **Furthermore,** students in class learn that their own interests do not always dictate activities and decisions. **Nevertheless,** proponents of home schooling argue that despite the socializing potential of classroom learning, the potential for intellectual growth is severely limited.

In this paragraph, you can see that the word *interaction,* repeated in the first two sentences, connects those sentences logically. The next two sentences begin with transitional words, *furthermore* and *nevertheless,* that show the relationship of the sentence to the one preceding it.

Writing a Conclusion

A concluding paragraph both sums up your paper and points to its significance. Some students are used to creating a conclusion by restating the introduction. In a short paper, however, a concluding paragraph need not

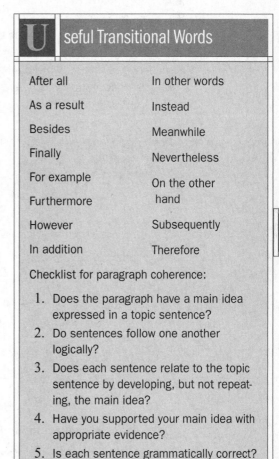

Useful Transitional Words

After all	In other words
As a result	Instead
Besides	Meanwhile
Finally	Nevertheless
For example	On the other hand
Furthermore	
However	Subsequently
In addition	Therefore

Checklist for paragraph coherence:

1. Does the paragraph have a main idea expressed in a topic sentence?
2. Do sentences follow one another logically?
3. Does each sentence relate to the topic sentence by developing, but not repeating, the main idea?
4. Have you supported your main idea with appropriate evidence?
5. Is each sentence grammatically correct?

8

repeat the assertions you made in your introduction. A more creative concluding paragraph might:

- suggest the implications of your ideas
- show how your topic is part of a larger issue
- suggest how your ideas can lead to changes in your readers' attitudes, behavior, or actions

REVISING

Revising means reseeing. Often, it's easier to "resee" your essay a day or two after you've written it. Writers call that waiting period a "cool down," when they have time to change their perspective from writer to reader. Revising can happen on two levels: globally, which means that you look at organization and paragraph construction; and locally, which means you look at sentences and words. If you decide to move a paragraph on the third page to the second page, you are revising globally. If you decide to restructure sentences to eliminate unnecessary words, or if you change particular word choices, then you are revising locally.

As you read your essay, use the following five questions to help you discover where you want to revise:

R evision Checklist

1. Does the essay have a clear focus?
2. Does the essay have a logical organization?
3. Is each paragraph organized around one main point? Do you support your main points with evidence?
4. Is your style appropriate for college-level work?
5. Is the essay technically and mechanically correct?

1. *Does the essay have a clear focus?*   You may have a clear idea of exactly what you intended to write about. Where is that idea clearly stated? To test whether the essay has a clear focus, read your first paragraphs and isolate the one or two sentences that give your main idea. Which sentences tell the reader what you are arguing? Which ones state the question you are answering or the problem you are trying to solve by writing this essay?

Your first paragraphs should help the reader to anticipate the structure of the essay: How will you answer your question? What sources will you examine? What texts will you discuss?

2. *Does the essay have a logical organization?*   An essay should not be an interior monologue, a record of your own stream of consciousness. To test whether your essay has a logical structure, construct an outline *from the essay*

itself. Number the paragraphs; write the main point of each paragraph in a single sentence. Do these sentences follow one another logically? Does each paragraph help to support your main idea? Should some paragraphs be reordered? Are any points missing?

An essay should have transitions between paragraphs. The last sentence of one paragraph should relate to the first sentence of the next paragraph. Sometimes, you can help your reader see the relationship between those sentences by including transitional words such as *therefore, however, finally, consequently, similarly.* If you find yourself beginning each paragraph with *also,* you should recognize that you are merely listing points rather than organizing them logically.

3. *Do you support your main points with evidence?*   Sometimes, you may find a paragraph where one idea is repeated in different ways in several sentences. That paragraph lacks development. Choose the sentence that best expresses your point, make that the topic sentence of the paragraph, and, in revising, find support for the point with concrete evidence from readings or research.

You should develop your essay by making assertions and supporting those assertions with evidence from your sources. Among your tasks in writing an essay are drawing inferences from the texts you are reading, showing connections between texts, identifying differences between texts, and tracing the development of ideas from early texts to later ones. All of these tasks require that you read texts carefully and use them as evidence. When you quote a text, your reader should understand why you are quoting, how you are reading the passage, and what ideas you are taking from it.

Your essay should reflect your ability to *think critically.* **Summarizing** (distilling the content of what you have read) and **observing** (noting certain patterns that recur in texts) are only beginning stages of critical thinking. Your reader wants to see that you can ask questions about texts, find key passages, draw inferences, and formulate your own argument.

4. *Is your style appropriate for college-level work?*   Some students try to impress their instructor by using cumbersome words and convoluted sentence structure. Big words, however, are not as important as strong ideas. Instructors prefer writing that is clear, lively, and concrete. On the other hand, they don't want slang or jargon. If you have doubts about your style, ask your instructor if you may see a successful paper written for the course by another student. Pay close attention to the style; you'll see that direct and precise language conveys ideas most clearly.

5. *Is the essay technically and mechanically correct?*   If you have problems with grammar or sentence correctness, Appendix A may help you learn some basic rules.

THREE QUALITIES TO AIM FOR IN YOUR WRITING

Good writing has conciseness, clarity, and coherence. Here are some guidelines for editing your own work to enhance these three qualities.

Conciseness

Conciseness does not necessarily mean brevity; it does mean that unnecessary words are eliminated. Strong writing depends on strong nouns and verbs. Compare the following sentences:

> A majority of staff members have the capability of contributing very mean-
> ingfully to policy decisions.

> Many staff members can contribute significantly to policy decisions.

The second sentence eliminates long phrases and empty words. A strong, concrete subject noun (members) takes the place of a weak, abstract subject noun (majority). A strong verb (can contribute) takes the place of a weak verb (have).

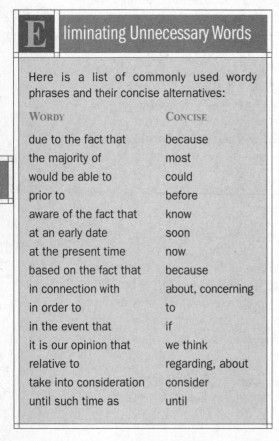

Eliminating Unnecessary Words

Here is a list of commonly used wordy phrases and their concise alternatives:

WORDY	CONCISE
due to the fact that	because
the majority of	most
would be able to	could
prior to	before
aware of the fact that	know
at an early date	soon
at the present time	now
based on the fact that	because
in connection with	about, concerning
in order to	to
in the event that	if
it is our opinion that	we think
relative to	regarding, about
take into consideration	consider
until such time as	until

Clarity

Clarity can be undermined by poor sentence structure or poor word choice. To check the clarity of a sentence, ask yourself: What is this sentence about? Do the subject and verb clearly indicate the sense of the sentence? To edit for better clarity, focus on the following:

- purpose
- subject
- verb
- construction
- word choice

Focus on the purpose. Sometimes the purpose is unclear:

It is the belief of the Accounting Department that the predicament was precipitated by a computational inaccuracy.

What is the purpose of this sentence? The writer seems to want to explain the cause of a problem. If so, the reader expects a sentence that reads: The problem was caused by this reason. Here is a revised sentence:

> The Accounting Department thinks the problem was caused by a computation error.

Focus on the subject. Sometimes, the real subject is hidden by poor construction:

> The use of this method of keeping records would promote increased efficiency.

In the sentence above, the subject is *use*. It is followed by two prepositional phrases (*of* this method, *of* keeping records) that are needed to clarify the word *use*. The actual subject of this sentence, however, is *method*. Here is a clearer sentence:

> This method of record-keeping would promote increased efficiency.

Focus on the verb. Sometimes, the real verb is hidden by poor construction:

> An investigation of all possible sources of funding was undertaken.

In this sentence, the passive verb form *was undertaken* obscures the real action of the sentence, which is the act of *investigating*. Here is a revised sentence:

> The department investigated all possible sources of funding.

Focus on construction. When the subject and verb are separated by long strings of phrases and clauses, the reader has trouble following the sense of the sentence:

> The bank, which had a long history of poor management and shaky investments, beginning in 1972 when a merger failed to strengthen its image in the banking world, and continuing to the present day, finally began to show signs of irreversible weakness during the present administration.

In this sentence, the subject *bank* is four lines away from the verb *began*. A revision would place the subject and verb closer to one another:

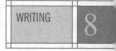

> The bank's long history of poor management and shaky investments began in 1972, when a merger failed to strengthen its image in the banking world. Under the present administration, the bank shows signs of irreversible weakness.

Focus on word choice. Your writing is as strong as the words you choose. Strong words are direct, lively, and precise; they are not necessarily polysyllabic, Latinate, and flowery:

> The organization endeavors to impact favorably upon the environment by promoting a recycling program to encompass all office waste materials.

A sentence with better word choice might be:

> The company's recycling program reflects its concern for the environment.

Some students worry that their vocabulary is too limited for college-level work. The best way to build a vocabulary is by reading. If you read challenging material, look up words you don't know. If you discover interesting words that you'd like to use in your own writing, keep a list with both the word and its use in context. Whatever you read, you'll grow in your facility with language.

As you write, you might struggle to find just the word you want. A quick way to jog your memory is by using the thesaurus or dictionary on your word-processing program. Click on Tools, then Language. You'll find Thesaurus as one of your options. A thesaurus is a compilation of synonyms. If you highlight any word in your own writing and click on Thesaurus, you'll find other choices that may be more appropriate. Experienced writers caution against using a thesaurus to choose a word you never have seen before just because it looks fancy. Words have connotations that often are revealed only when you know how they are used in context. The thesaurus option also includes a dictionary, so you can check the meaning of a word you may not be sure about.

Coherence

In writing, coherence means that one sentence relates logically to the next. Transitional words, when necessary, help the reader to understand the relationship among sentences. In one paragraph, all sentences develop one idea; no information is missing, and no irrelevant information is included. Here are two sentences that lack coherence:

> Because the company was concerned about contract forms, it hired a law
> firm to review them. There have been many changes in contract law during
> the last 10 years, and the company discovered that its forms were obsolete.

These two sentences seem choppy because they are not logically connected. The end of the first sentence does not lead the reader into the second sentence. The second sentence begins with an idea that is only hinted at in the first sentence. Through revised sentence structure or the use of transitions, a writer can help readers understand the logic of the writing:

> The law firm advised the company to change its contract forms. Those
> forms, in use for a decade, were now outdated because of major changes in
> contract law.

WORD PROCESSING

Computers make writing deceptively easy, because instead of typing an essay over and over as you move from draft to revision, you can cut and paste, delete passages with the press of a key, change fonts at will, and print out a piece of work that looks clean, neat and professional. Experienced writers, though, report that they edit both on screen and on hard copies. They don't rely on some computer functions—spell checkers, for example, or grammar checkers, to insure correctness.

Computers do make some tasks easier:

- You can create lists identified by bullet points or numbers. This function appears on the Tool Bar.
- You can number pages. Click on Insert, then Page Numbers for options.
- You can change spacing, margins, and fonts. Click on Format.
- You can insert endnotes or footnotes. Click on Insert, then Reference, then Footnote. When you type your information, the note will automatically be entered at the bottom of the page or the end of your document.
- You can import a passage from a text or note file into your current work. For example, if you take notes on a computer, you can highlight a passage, click on Edit, click on Cut or Copy and close your file. Open your essay, locate the place you want to insert the passage, and click on Paste.
- You can replace words throughout an essay by asking your computer to find a word and replace it with another. Click on Edit, then Replace. This function is useful if you decide that one word is more appropriate than something you have chosen to use; or if you decide that you over-use a word and want to replace it with another word.
- You can find word choices or meanings by clicking on Tools, then Language, and then on the Thesaurus or Dictionary option.
- You can edit your essay or ask someone else to edit your essay and indicate suggested changes using Track Changes, an option under Tools. This function highlights suggestions in a bright color, making them visible as you read through your essay.

Tips for Writing on a Computer

1. Save your work often. Back up your drafts during the writing process as well as at the end of each writing session. "My computer crashed" is an excuse your professors are tired of hearing.
2. Proofread carefully. Don't rely on spell checkers or grammar checkers to correct your errors. Neither tool can understand the cents of your own sentences. Or do I mean sense? Neither a spell checker nor grammar checker found "cents" to be an error. After all, it's spelled correctly and it's a noun. You need to take responsibility for correctness.
3. After cutting and pasting passages, make sure the material reads logically. Students often cut and paste without creating needed transitions or other logical connections.
4. Give your revisions a clear file name so you don't hand in an early draft by mistake.
5. Print out your work for a final editing. Experienced writers often find mistakes on a hard copy that they missed when reading on the screen.

8

Writing is a challenge for all writers, even professionals. No one sits down at a computer and produces a perfect piece of writing. Instead, writing is the product of much thinking, questioning, and revising. It is an ongoing process that reflects the learning and growth you will experience as you progress through college.

GRAMMAR BRUSHUP

ost of us learned principles of grammar far back in our school careers. This chapter will remind you of what you may already know, teach you some things you may not know, and serve as a reference for revising your work.

THE PARTS OF SPEECH

The parts of speech are the names of words that perform different functions in our language.

NOUN. A **noun** names a person, animal, place, object, or idea:

> Edward
> psychology
> the Empire State Building

These words all are nouns.

PRONOUN. A **pronoun** takes the place of a noun and may be singular or plural:

> *Singular:* I, you, he, she, it
> *Plural:* we, you, they

Pronouns, like nouns, may show possession. Possessive pronouns are:

> *Singular:* my, mine, your, yours, her, hers, his, its
> *Plural:* our, ours, your, yours, their, theirs

VERB. A **verb** describes action, shows a state of being, or helps other verbs. These verbs show action:

> tumble
> accelerate
> invent

Verbs that show a state of being include *is, are, was*, and *were:*

> Edward *is* nine.

In this example, *is,* a form of *to be,* expresses Edward's age, not something that Edward is doing.

In the examples below, forms of *have* and *be* serve as helping verbs:

> The psychologist *has* studied extrasensory perception.
> His work *is* published regularly in professional journals.

ADJECTIVE. An **adjective** describes a noun or pronoun:

> the *unruly* child
> an *intense* argument

ADVERB. An **adverb** describes a verb, an adjective, or another adverb:

> The carpenter worked *carefully.*
> My instructor gave directions *too quickly.*

Carefully and *quickly* describe verbs; *too* describes another adverb.

PREPOSITION. A **preposition** is a word that can be joined with a noun to function as an adjective or adverb:

> The book *on* the table is my textbook.
> The man *without* a hat is my husband.

GRAMMAR
BRUSHUP

Some common prepositions include:

about	above	across
after	against	along (or along with)
among	around	as
at	before	behind
below	beneath	beside
besides	between	beyond
by	despite	during
except	for	from
in	inside	into
near	next	of

on	out	over
since	through	to
under	until	up
upon	with	within
without		

CONJUNCTION. A **conjunction** joins words, phrases, or clauses:

Political Science *and* Psychology are my favorite classes this semester.
I arrived late, *but* the lecture had not yet started.

The most common conjunctions are:

and, but, for, nor, or, so, yet

Other conjunctions come in pairs:

both—and
either—or
neither—nor
not only—but also
whether—or

Here are two examples:

Neither the state legislature *nor* the federal government opposed the new law.
Both Vermont *and* Massachusetts support recycling.

WHAT IS A SENTENCE?

A **sentence** is a group of words that contains a *subject* (a noun) and a *predicate* (a verb) and makes sense alone. Another term for *sentence* is *independent clause.* Consider two examples:

GRAMMAR
BRUSHUP   A

The boy laughed.
The attorney, in practice for 10 years, presented an argument in defense of his client.

The first example is a sentence because it contains a subject (the boy) and a predicate (laughed). The subject contains a noun; the predicate in this case is a verb. You know both who did something and what was done.

The second example contains the same elements: a subject (the attorney) and a predicate (presented an argument). In this sentence, the verb *presented* takes an object, *argument,* that tells us what the attorney presented.

Sentence Fragments

A **sentence fragment** is a group of words that does not make sense alone because it lacks either a subject or a verb, or because it contains a word or phrase that makes it a *dependent clause* (it is dependent on additional words in order to make sense). Here are three examples:

> Under the new law in effect since October.
> For example, courses with no midterm or final exam.
> Despite the author's argument about the comparative economic strength of both economies.

In the third example, the word *despite* signals the beginning of a dependent clause. This clause can serve as the beginning of a sentence:

> Despite the author's argument about the comparative economic strength of both economies, the book fails to present a clear forecast of future growth.

In this sentence, the subject is *book* and the verb is *fails*. This subject and verb make the passage a sentence.

Combined Sentences

To keep our writing from being choppy, we often combine sentences. The simplest way to combine sentences is by using a comma followed by a conjunction: *and, but, for, nor, or, so, yet*. For example:

> Rain drenched the garden, *and* the flowers grew.
> I will take the train, *or* I will wait for the bus.
> I tried to reach you, *but* your phone was turned off.

There is a complete sentence on either side of each conjunction.

The *semicolon* may be used instead of a conjunction to combine complete sentences:

> I may take the train; on the other hand, I may wait for the bus.

Another, more sophisticated way of combining sentences is to turn one part of the sentence into a dependent clause. A **dependent clause** may contain a subject and a verb, but it is not a complete sentence because it is introduced by a preposition (or a prepositional phrase) or an adverb (or an adverbial phrase). Consider these two examples:

1. I tried to reach you. I discovered your phone was turned off.
   When I tried to reach you, I discovered your phone was turned off.
2. Rain drenches the garden. The flowers will grow.
   After rain drenches the garden, the flowers will grow.

In these two examples, the words in italics form a clause. That clause cannot stand independently; it is not a sentence.

Run-On Sentences and Comma Splices

When two sentences are incorrectly combined, the result is a run-on sentence or a comma splice. A comma alone cannot serve as a connector between two sentences. For example:

> The author argues about the strength of both economies, the book fails to present a clear forecast of future growth.

When a comma is used incorrectly to combine sentences, the error is called a **comma splice**. When the comma is omitted altogether, the error is called a **run-on sentence**.

To correctly combine the two sentences in the example, you may add the word *but* after the comma:

> The author argues about the strength of both economies, but the book fails to present a clear forecast of future growth.

Another way of combining these two sentences is by using a semicolon and a transitional phrase:

> The author argues about the strength of both economies; nevertheless, the book fails to present a clear forecast of future growth.

PRONOUN PROTOCOL

When you substitute a pronoun for a noun, your reader needs to know precisely what noun is being replaced. For example:

> The boy is 15, and he is tall for his age.

GRAMMAR BRUSHUP | A

The word *he* is a pronoun in this sentence, replacing the noun *boy*.

Sometimes, the reference is not as clear as in the example. The following sentence does not show a clear referent for the pronoun *it:*

> Whenever an economic indicator points to a possible problem, it causes a reaction in government.

What causes the reaction: the indicator or the problem? This sentence needs to be restructured as follows to avoid confusion:

> Whenever an economic indicator points to a possible problem, government reacts.

Noun and Pronoun Agreement

Singular nouns need to be replaced by singular pronouns, plural nouns by plural pronouns:

> *Singular:* The lecturer presented new ideas to the audience. He made sure that he defined all his key terms.
>
> *Plural:* The speakers on the panel were well informed about campaign strategies, based on their own experiences.

The following sentence, however, reveals a common problem:

> Each speaker was well informed about campaign strategies, based on their own experiences.

The noun *speaker* is singular; the pronoun *their* is plural. Therefore, the sentence is grammatically incorrect.

Making the sentence correct, however, poses another problem: The speakers on the panel included two women and two men. Here is another sentence:

> Each speaker was well informed about campaign strategies, based on his or her own experiences.

This correction, however, is wordy.

Using a plural noun in this sentence avoids both wordiness and the problem of using pronouns that designate gender:

> The speakers were well informed about campaign strategies, based on their own experiences.

HANDLING VERBS

A   GRAMMAR
     BRUSHUP

Subject–Verb Agreement

Just as nouns and pronouns must agree in number, subjects and verbs must agree in number (singular or plural) and person (first, second, or third):

> *Singular:* The poll shows that the Democratic candidate has a 20-percent lead.

Poll is a noun in the third-person singular. Singular verbs in the third person generally end in *s*.

> *Plural:* The polls indicate a healthy lead for our candidate.

Polls is a noun in the third-person plural. Plural verbs in the third person generally do not end in *s*.

As with nouns and pronouns, sometimes agreement problems occur, as in the following case:

Incorrect: Three polls were taken. *Each* of the polls *show* a substantial margin of victory.

Even though three polls were taken, in the second sentence, you are indicating the results of each single poll. *Each* is the subject of the sentence; because it is singular, it must take a singular verb.

Verb Parts

Sometimes, a verb is just one word in a sentence:

The boy *jumped* from the ledge.

Here, the verb is *jumped.*
Sometimes, however, the verb is more than one word:

The boy *had jumped* from the ledge before his father came to help him.

Here, the verb is two words: *had jumped.* Generally, a sentence is clearer if the words that make up a verb are not interrupted by other words.
Some instructors insist on following two grammatical conventions:

1. Don't split infinitives. An **infinitive** is a verb form that begins with *to:* to go, to see, to plummet.
   Incorrect: He decided to finally go to Europe.
   Correct: He finally decided to go to Europe.
                   Finally, he decided to go to Europe.
                   He decided finally to go to Europe.
2. Don't split verb parts. Some verbs consist of several words: have been ill, was going, has taken.
   Incorrect: He *could* definitely *have avoided* the mistake by doing nothing.
   Correct: He definitely *could have avoided* the mistake by doing nothing.

GRAMMAR
BRUSHUP   A

PLACING PHRASES AND CLAUSES LOGICALLY

To avoid confusion, place phrases and clauses near the words they modify:

Confusing: Religious intolerance caused waves of emigration toward dissenters.

In this sentence, the phrase *toward dissenters* should modify *religious intolerance*. Here is the restructured sentence:

Clear: Religious intolerance toward dissenters caused waves of emigration.

In the following sentence, the phrase *from Oxford University* describes the noun *speaker:*

The speaker who delivered the opening address, from Oxford University, generated hearty applause.

As the sentence is constructed, it sounds as if either the opening address came from Oxford University or the speaker delivered the address while at Oxford University.

Placing the phrase next to the noun it modifies avoids this kind of confusion:

The speaker from Oxford University, who delivered the opening address, generated hearty applause.

Modifiers must refer to a word in the sentence; if they do not, they are called **dangling modifiers.** The sentence below has a dangling modifier and needs to be reconstructed:

Drawing upon campaign experiences, the audience listened attentively to the speaker.

However, it was the speaker, not the audience, who drew upon campaign experiences. Here is a revised sentence:

Drawing upon campaign experiences, the speaker captivated the audience.

PUNCTUATION

Comma

The **comma** is a useful form of punctuation because it helps you write clearly by separating parts of a sentence from other parts. The main uses for the comma are:

- to work along with a conjunction that joins two complete sentences

  The book is difficult, but I understand most of it.

- to separate items in a series

  The author discusses social, cultural, and personal influences on behavior.

- to set off an introductory word or phrase

  Usually, there are no obstacles to success.

- to set off a nonrestrictive phrase or clause from the rest of the sentence

Ronald Reagan, a Republican President, made substantial economic reforms.

In the last example, the phrase a *Republican President* is **nonrestrictive:** It is not necessary for the reader or the sense of the sentence. The writer assumes that the reader knows who Reagan is and cites Reagan's political affiliation simply as additional information.

If the reader does need the information in the phrase or clause, then the phrase or clause is **restrictive.**

The speaker who advised Reagan provided useful background information about the current crisis.

In this sentence, readers need to know *which* speaker the writer is referring to; he is, specifically, *the speaker who advised Reagan.* That information, which is necessary for the sense of the sentence, is included in a restrictive, or necessary, clause.

Two other uses for commas are:

- to set off direct quotations

"Bring me the book," he demanded.

(Notice here that the comma goes *inside* the quotation marks.)

- in dates and addresses

On June 4, 1992, my sister graduated from college in Washington, D.C.

Semicolon

Semicolons serve two main purposes:

- to separate items in a series when one or more items contain a comma

The panel included John Allen, last year's award winner; Preston Smith; and this year's award winner, Marian Copley.

- to join two sentences when no conjunction is used to connect them

The reception convened at 10; nevertheless, a few people still came late.

Remember: Nevertheless cannot join two independent clauses unless a semicolon is used. Neither can other transitional words, such as:

furthermore	then	however	therefore
likewise	thus	similarly	

Quotation Marks

Quotation marks enclose the exact words of a speaker or writer. Notice how a quotation by novelist Katherine Anne Porter is used in different ways by different writers. First, the quotation is unbroken:

> As Katherine Anne Porter wrote, "Most people won't realize that writing is a craft. You have to take your apprenticeship in it like anything else."

In the next example, breaking the quotation makes for a more conversational tone:

> "Most people won't realize that writing is a craft," said the novelist Katherine Anne Porter. "You have to take your apprenticeship in it like anything else."

Next, excerpts from the quotation are used:

> Katherine Anne Porter called writing "a craft" that requires an "apprenticeship . . . like anything else."

In this example, notice the use of three dots to signify the omission of words from the original quotation; these dots are called an **ellipsis**.

In the fourth example, the end of the quotation is left out:

> Katherine Anne Porter saw writing as "a craft" and advised beginning writers "to take your apprenticeship in it. . . ."

Here, notice that there are four dots at the end of quoted material: Three dots signify an ellipsis; one dot is the period for the sentence.

Quotation marks are also used to enclose the titles of short poems, short stories, magazine or newspaper articles, essays, television episodes, and chapter titles:

> Yesterday's editorial, "Medicare Medicine," offered some concrete suggestions for reform.

Place commas and periods *inside* quotation marks; place semicolons and colons *outside* quotation marks. *Remember:* The end punctuation in the original quotation is dropped in favor of the punctuation you need for the correctness of your sentence. Suppose you wanted to quote the following sentence by Robert Louis Stevenson: "The difficulty of literature is not to write, but to write what you mean." Here is one possible sentence:

> "The difficulty of literature is not to write, but to write what you mean," said Stevenson.

In this example, the end punctuation of the quotation, a period, is dropped. A comma, necessary for your sentence, is inserted instead. Notice that the comma goes *inside* the quotation marks.

USING THE ACTIVE VOICE

Nouns and verbs are important parts of speech. More than other words, they convey the sense of what you want to say. When you use the **active voice**, the subject of the sentence acts; the verb describes that action:

> The candidate announced his platform last week.

In this sentence, the subject, *candidate,* took action: He announced his ideas.
When you use the **passive voice,** the subject of the sentence is acted upon:

> The platform was announced last week.

In this sentence, the subject *platform* is not taking action; it is acted upon. But by whom? Who announced the platform? The sentence does not tell us.
Because passive construction omits the real subject of the sentence, its use makes writing confusing and weak. Sometimes, students use the passive construction when they feel uncomfortable about making their own argument.

POSSESSIVES

The people or things that nouns represent are able to possess or own. An apostrophe followed by an *s* indicates possession:

> Robert's lecture was more interesting than John's.
> James Joyce's *Ulysses* was the text for my English class.

Pronouns also are able to show possession, but possessive pronouns are not formed by adding an apostrophe and an *s.* See "The Parts of Speech" for a list of possessive pronouns.

COMMON USAGE ERRORS

GRAMMAR
BRUSHUP   A

This section focuses on commonly confused words; it is designed to help you choose the correct word for your sentence.

ACCEPT, EXCEPT. *Accept* means to receive or agree to; *except* means *but:*

- The applicant decided to accept the position.
- Everyone except John went on the trip.

AFFECT, EFFECT. *Affect,* a verb, means to change or influence; *effect,* a noun, means result:

- The war affected women's job opportunities.
- The effect of the war can be seen in the current workforce.

AGGRAVATE, IRRITATE. *Aggravate* means to make worse; *irritate* means to annoy:

- The noisy children aggravated my headache.
- The noisy children irritated their grandfather.

ALL READY, ALREADY. *All ready* means prepared; *already* means previously:

- We were all ready to go on the trip.
- The tickets already had arrived.

ALL RIGHT. *All right* is always two words:

- Our plans were all right with my parents.

ALLUSION, ILLUSION. *Allusion* is an indirect reference to something; *illusion* is an image or appearance:

- The horror film contained allusions to *Frankenstein* and *Dracula*.
- When the monster appeared, the victims at first thought they were perceiving an illusion.

A LOT. *A lot,* meaning *much,* usually is too colloquial an expression for a college essay; *alot* is incorrect.

AMONG, BETWEEN. *Among* is appropriate when the emphasis is on distribution rather than individual relationships; *between* is used to denote a one-to-one relationship, regardless of the number of items; it can be used when the number is unspecified or when more than two items are enumerated:

- I had to choose a partner from among my best friends.
- Finally, I chose between Sue and Mary.

AMOUNT, NUMBER. *Amount* refers to quantities that you cannot count; *number* refers to objects you can count:

- A large amount of food is needed for the starving people of Uganda.
- A number of charitable organizations have decided to contribute.

ANYONE, ANY ONE. *Anyone* means any person; *any one* means any single person or thing:

- Anyone can attend the conference.
- Any one of the speakers can answer your question.

BAD, BADLY. *Bad* is an adjective (it must describe a noun); *badly* is an adverb (it must describe a verb, an adjective, or another adverb):

- The bad apple was moldy.
- The pianist performed badly on Friday night.

BESIDE, BESIDES. *Beside* means next to; *besides* means in addition to or moreover:

- The moderator sat beside the main speaker.
- Besides making a clear argument, he gave strong examples.

CAN, MAY. *Can* refers to the ability to do something; *may* refers to permission to do something or to the possibility that something may occur:

- Because he was trained in carpentry, Bill can build a house.
- Bill may build a house on our property.

COMPLEMENT, COMPLIMENT. *Complement* means to complete or enhance; *compliment* is a flattering remark:

- Hiring an accountant complements our support staff.
- The professor complimented my latest essay.

CONSCIENCE, CONSCIOUS. *Conscience* allows us to distinguish between right and wrong; *conscious* means aware of or alert:

- His conscience told him not to cheat.
- He was conscious of his parents' influence.

CONTINUAL, CONTINUOUS. *Continual* refers to the repetition of an activity; *continuous* means without interruption:

- His continual failure on math tests caused him to hire a tutor.
- Yesterday's continuous rain caused flooding.

COUNCIL, COUNSEL. *Council* means a group of people; *counsel* can be a noun, meaning advice, or a verb, meaning to advise:

- The mayor's council established a youth club.
- The club's director counseled members.

CRITERIA, CRITERION. *Criteria* is the plural of *criterion,* meaning basis of judgment:

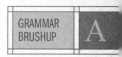

GRAMMAR BRUSHUP A

- The most important criterion for hiring a teacher is the ability to make ideas clear.

DATA. *Data* is the plural of *datum,* meaning fact:

- The data collected by the researchers support adopting a new method of experimentation.

Note: Because *data* is a plural noun, it takes a plural form of the verb.

DIFFERENT FROM. The preposition *from* is the correct word to use with *different:*

- My version of the report is different from yours.

DISINTERESTED, UNINTERESTED. *Disinterested* means unbiased; *uninterested* means not interested:

- We brought the problem to a disinterested mediator.
- The mayor was uninterested in solving the problem himself.

EXPLICIT, IMPLICIT. *Explicit* means fully expressed; *implicit* means implied:

- The contract explicitly stated our responsibilities.
- Close analysis sometimes reveals the implicit meaning of a poem.

FARTHER, FURTHER. *Farther* refers to physical distance; *further* means more or additional:

- You need to go farther down the road to find the restaurant.
- He argued further to convince me to accept his position.

FEWER, LESS. *Fewer* refers to things you can count; *less* refers to things that are not countable:

- He brought fewer supplies to the laboratory than I did.
- I had less difficulty completing the lab experiment.

GOOD, WELL. *Good* is an adjective; *well* can be either an adjective (meaning in good health) or an adverb (meaning in a good manner, skillfully):

- We had good weather for the picnic.
- The boys played volleyball well.

IMPLY, INFER. *Imply* means to suggest; *infer* means to draw a conclusion from something:

- His behavior implied his attitude toward the group.
- We inferred that he wished he were not participating.

ITS, IT'S. *Its* is a possessive of the pronoun *it; it's* is a contraction of *it is:*

- The wind knocked the statue off its pedestal.
- It's unusual to have such a storm.

LAY, LIE. *Lay* means to put something down or to place an object (the past tense of *lay* is *laid*); *lie* means to recline (the past tense of *lie* is *lay*):

- Be careful when you lay the crystal bowl on the table.
- My cousin lay on the beach for the whole vacation.

LIKE, AS. *Like* should be followed by a noun (or noun phrase); *as* should be followed by a clause containing a subject and verb:

- The child looks like his father.
- The musician played the Bach fugue as it ought to be played.

LOOSE, LOSE. *Loose* means unfastened; *lose* means to misplace:

- The awning became loose and began to fall.
- Watch your belongings so you don't lose anything.

MEDIA, MEDIUM. *Media* is the plural of *medium,* which refers to a means or mode:

- The media reported the bombing in great detail.
- Television, though, seemed the most suitable medium to convey enough information.

PRECEDE, PROCEED. *Precede* means to go before; *proceed* means to move forward:

- The main speaker preceded the rest of the panel.
- The committee will proceed on my application as soon as it is complete.

PRINCIPAL, PRINCIPLE. *Principal* means the director of a school or the first (or highest) in rank; *principle* means rule or theory:

- The principal attraction of New York City is its theaters.
- Cheating goes against my principles of ethical behavior.

STATIONERY, STATIONARY. *Stationery* means writing paper; *stationary* means fixed in place:

- My stationery is imprinted with my name and address.
- The old warship remained stationary in the harbor.

THAN, THEN. *Than* can be a conjunction or a preposition, referring to a comparison; *then* is an adverb referring to time:

- The student would prefer to take a written test than to take an oral exam.
- After we complete the questionnaire, then we can leave.

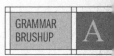

GRAMMAR
BRUSHUP
A

WHO, WHOM. *Who* is a subjective pronoun (it replaces a subject in a sentence); *whom* is an objective pronoun (it replaces an object in a sentence):

- I saw the actor who performed last night.
- Let me know to whom I should send this letter.

WHO'S, WHOSE. *Who's* is a contraction for *who is* or *who has; whose* is a possessive adjective:

- Who's attending the concert tonight?
- Whose tickets were left in the reception room?

YOUR, YOU'RE. *Your* is a possessive adjective; *you're* is a contraction for *you are:*

- Your talk was the best on the panel.
- You're going to be invited to another conference.

This brief grammar review may help you to correct some problems as you write your college essays. Most students find it helpful to have a grammar handbook on their bookshelf. See "Additional Resources" for some popular and widely used handbooks.

ADDITIONAL RESOURCES

Hacker, Diane. *A Writer's Handbook*, 4th ed. Boston: Bedford Books, 2000.

Harris, Muriel. *Prentice Hall Reference Guide to Grammar and Usage,* 6th ed. Upper Saddle River, NJ: Prentice Hall, 2005.

Troyka, Lynn Quitman. *Simon & Schuster Quick Access Reference for Writers,* 3rd ed. Upper Saddle River, NJ: Prentice Hall, 2000.

A | GRAMMAR BRUSHUP

MATH BRUSHUP

he level of mathematical literacy needed to participate in the world—its jobs, its economic and social orders, and its democratic institutions—has risen dramatically in the last decades. Today, the ability to understand quantitative issues that involve mathematics, science, and technology is a critical skill for all citizens. Environmental and fiscal policy issues facing us today will profoundly affect the future livability of this planet and our future quality of life. In our modern information age, everyone needs a basic understanding of mathematics.

This appendix reviews some of the basics of math, including arithmetic, multiplication, fractions, decimals and percentages, scientific notation, algebra, exponents, and ratios. The appendix also gives you a strategy for dealing with word problems. Your instructor may choose to cover this material in class, or, alternatively, to refer you to this material to cover on your own. If you currently are taking a math course, the material may reinforce what you are learning in your class.

Before we turn to the math topics, let's take a look at the issue of mathematics anxiety, which so many people face.

MATH ANXIETY IS A LEARNED BEHAVIOR

Traditionally, basic mathematics courses have focused on developing the skills that are required for the next mathematics course. Because real-world applications require complex calculations, traditional courses have restricted the problems students are asked to solve to simple applications—applications designed to illustrate mathematical topics, not real-world issues. With mathematics taught in this way, it is no wonder many people have developed a dislike of mathematics. In such courses, students often develop the opinion that mathematics is not personally relevant and that "word problems" are puzzles contrived to frustrate students rather than the reason for learning mathematics.

Research shows that the following misconceptions about mathematics are common*:

- Mathematics is a collection of rules and procedures.
- Mathematics problems have one and only one right answer.
- There is only one correct way to solve any mathematics problem—usually the rule the teacher has most recently demonstrated to the class.
- Ordinary students cannot expect to understand mathematics; they expect to simply memorize it and apply, mechanically and without understanding, what they have learned.
- Mathematics is a solitary activity, done by individuals in isolation.
- Students who have understood the mathematics they have studied will be able to solve any assigned problem in five minutes or less.

If you hold any of the above beliefs, you're likely to have at least a slight case of mathematics anxiety, a term used to describe negative feelings toward mathematics that vary in intensity from a dislike or avoidance of mathematics to a state of panic, helplessness, and paralysis. There is nothing wrong with you for having mathematics anxiety; in fact, it is often a completely appropriate response.

How does the desire to succeed at math lead to anxiety that causes one to fail? Through a natural process of association: It is both natural and logical that if two items often have occurred together, then whenever one occurs, the other will likely occur as well. The Russian physiologist Ivan Pavlov spent years studying this type of association after he observed that the dogs in his laboratory had learned to salivate in response to a bell that preceded their being fed. Dogs naturally salivate when food is presented, but Pavlov's dogs learned to *anticipate* that food would be presented when the bell rang. This type of learning, known as *conditioning,* teaches people math anxiety.

If you hold beliefs that limit your success with mathematics, then you may perform at less than your best, resulting in feelings of inferiority, inadequacy, fear, and anxiety. It is only natural that if you are unsuccessful at mathematics

*A. H. Schoenfeld, "Learning to Think Mathematically: Problem Solving, Metacognition, and Sense Making in Mathematics," in *Handbook of Research on Mathematics Teaching and Learning*, ed. D. A. Grouws. New York: Macmillan, 1992: 334–70.

despite determined, repeated efforts, you will grow to dislike and avoid mathematics. We all learn to avoid things that make us feel bad.

OVERCOMING MATHEMATICS ANXIETY

If you have math anxiety, admit it. If you pretend not to have it, you will not learn to overcome or manage it. Think back on your previous experiences with mathematics. Do you remember when you first developed the feeling that you weren't good at math? Most students who have math anxiety can recall a particular math class where they first experienced their anxiety. Often, they can recall being called upon to present to the class solutions they didn't have.

Numerous relaxation techniques can help you learn to control your anxiety if it is acute; but to truly overcome your anxiety, you need to learn to value and to be successful with mathematics. Though that is a tall order, there are many strategies, including those listed below.

- Discover your particular learning style. Are you a visual, auditory, or kinesthetic/tactile learner? Determine for yourself how time of day, sound, lighting, temperature, food intake, and social environment affect your learning.
- Practice effective math study skills. Read your text with a pencil in hand. When you see a formula, plug in numbers to make sure you know how to use it.
- Carefully select your math class and your teacher. The way your teacher presents material can make a difference in your learning.
- Get involved in the learning process; don't be passive. Go to class regularly and sit near the front of class. Take careful notes and go over them each day shortly after class. Stay current; don't fall behind.
- Make sure your study setting is free from distractions. Organize your time and stick closely to your plan. Allow time for recreation and study breaks. When you are to study, study; when you schedule yourself to have fun, relax and enjoy yourself.

THE LANGUAGE OF MATHEMATICS

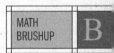

MATH
BRUSHUP   B

Often, the difficulty that students have in higher-level mathematics courses results from not having learned (or having forgotten) essential math skills. You cannot be successful with higher-level mathematics if you don't have a good grasp of the basics. Don't think, "I couldn't learn it before, so I can't learn it now." It's never too late to learn.

We will begin our review of mathematics at its origins. Human beings first began to use tools about 35,000 years ago. These early people were primarily nomadic hunters, dependent on migrating herds of animals for their survival. These early humans kept numerical records by notching sticks and bones called **tally sticks**. On a tally stick, notches are made to represent objects, so that ||| represents 3, |||| 4, etc. Tallies were the first use of mathematics. As simple as the idea seems, keeping a tally requires forming a correspondence between a set of objects, such as a herd of deer or days since the last snow, and an abstract representation of those objects.

As the need to count large numbers grew, an improved version of the system gathered the notches into groups of five, making it much easier to count large numbers. For example, it is much easier to tell that ||||| ||||| ||||| ||||| ||||| || represents 27 than |||||||||||||||||||||||||||. The numbers that can be represented by tally marks are called the **counting** or **whole numbers**. The grouping of tally marks into groups of five—rather than four, six, or some other choice—is natural because we have five fingers on each hand and five toes on each foot. The process of grouping and introducing a new symbol to represent the group is the most basic process in the development of numeral systems. The Roman system, for example, uses I for 1, V for 5, X for 10, etc. This is the same idea used in currency. You deal with a variety of different groupings of money every day: pennies, nickels, dimes, dollars, 5-dollar bills, 10-dollar bills, etc.

Although more efficient than the tally system, it is very cumbersome to represent large numbers in such a system—one is constantly having to introduce new symbols. Our modern numeral system, called the Arabic or Hindu–Arabic

Tally	Roman	Hindu–Arabic	Modern Currency Equivalent
ⱴ (100 groups of five)	D	500	Five-dollar bill
(20 groups of five)	C	100	Dollar bill
(10 groups of five)	L	50	50-cent piece
﷼﷼ (2 groups of five)	X	10	Dime
﷼ (1 group of five)	V	5	Nickel
|	I	1	Penny

numeral system, avoids having to introduce new symbols for larger numbers because it is positional. In our system, only nine numerals and a place holder, 0, are needed to represent any number because the units represented by each numeral increase by a power of 10 as we read from right to left. When we write 23, the 2 and the 3 are associated with different units. By 23, we mean 2 groups of ten and 3 ones. By 467, we mean 4 groups of one hundred, 6 groups of ten, and 7 ones.

ARITHMETIC

Fundamental to the concept of number is **arithmetic**, which encompasses the concepts of counting, addition, and subtraction. When we add one object to a set, it increases the number of objects in the set by one; similarly, removing one object decreases the size by one. In a tally system, to add two numbers means a person simply combined the tally marks. Subtraction was carried out by removing the appropriate number of tally marks.

Mastering our modern system is a little more difficult because the system is positional. Because each position represents a different size, we only can add or subtract numerals in like positions. To add 12 to 34, for example, we add the 1 and the 3 together because these represent groups of ten, and the 2 and the 4 because these represent single units.

$$\begin{array}{r} 12 \\ + 34 \\ \hline 46 \end{array}$$

Adding and subtracting often require converting from one position to an adjacent one, a procedure called **carrying**. Consider 5 plus 6, for example. When we add the digits in the ones position (5 and 6), the result is larger than 10, so we carry from the ones position to the tens position.

$$\begin{array}{r} 5 \\ + 6 \\ \hline 11 \end{array}$$

A similar situation occurs when we subtract. For example, to subtract 14 from 33 we first must convert 1 of the 3 tens in 33 to 10 ones $(33 = 13 + 20)$. We subtract 4 ones from 13 ones, leaving 9. Then, to complete the operation, we subtract 1 ten from the 2 tens remaining (in 33), leaving 1 ten. The final result is 1 ten and 9 ones, 19.

$$\begin{array}{r} 33 \\ - 14 \\ \hline 19 \end{array}$$

MULTIPLICATION

Multiplication can be viewed either as repeated addition or as the number of blocks in a grid with appropriate dimensions. For example, 7 times 4 (denoted 7 * 4),* can be thought of as 7 rows of 4 blocks, or 4 rows of 7 blocks. Rearranging these blocks into groups of 10, we have 2 groups of 10 with 8 left

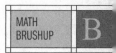

MATH BRUSHUP   B

---

*In this text, we will use * to denote multiplication rather than ×, which is often confused with the variable *x*.

over, for a total of 28 objects. The result of multiplying two numbers together is the **product**. So, in this case, 4 * 7 = 28; 28 is the product.

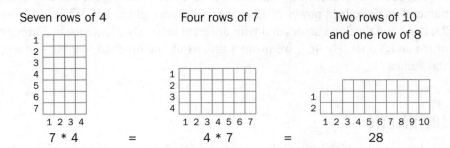

Seven rows of 4   Four rows of 7   Two rows of 10 and one row of 8

7 * 4   =   4 * 7   =   28

In the example above, each block represents a single object, but often it is convenient to have each block represent a group of 10, 100, or even 1,000 objects. For example, rather than represent the product of 7 times 300 by drawing a grid of 7 rows and 300 columns, we simply draw a grid with three columns, letting each block represent 100:

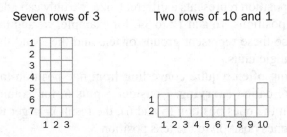

Seven rows of 3   Two rows of 10 and 1

There are 21 blocks, each representing 100 objects, so the product of 7 times 300 is 21 groups of hundreds. That is, 7 * 300 = 2,100.

Visualizing a grid helps us understand multiplication. However, to actually carry out calculations, we memorize times tables and a procedure to reduce complex multiplications to a series of smaller multiplications and additions. Consider 17 times 34. Because 17 is 7 ones and 1 ten, to multiply 17 by 34, we add the results of multiplying 7 by 34 and 10 by 34. Each of these multiplications can be split by noting that 34 is 4 ones and 30. Thus, 17 times 34 can be calculated by adding 7 * 4, 7 * 30, 10 * 4, and 10 * 30:

B   MATH BRUSHUP

$$
\begin{array}{rcrcrcrcr}
 & & & & & & & & 28 \\
 & & & & & & & & 210 \\
 & & 7 & & 7 & & 10 & & 10 & & 40 \\
17 & & & & & & & & \\
* \ 34 & = & * \ 4 & + & * \ 30 & + & * \ 4 & + & * \ 30 & = & +300 \\
 & & 28 & & 210 & & 40 & & 300 & & 578
\end{array}
$$

The shorthand method for this calculation proceeds with the same steps but uses less space:

```
       2
      17          17          17          17          17
    * 34    →    * 34   →    * 34   →    * 34   →    * 34
    ————         ————        ————        ————        ————
      8           238         238         238         238
                              40          340        +340
                                                     ————
                                                      578
```

FRACTIONS

If we understand the process of dividing something into pieces of equal size, we can think of any **fraction** as composed of a certain number of these pieces. For example, consider the fraction ⅚. Visualize this fraction by imagining an object, say a pie, cut into six equal pieces. The fraction ⅚ represents five of the six pieces:

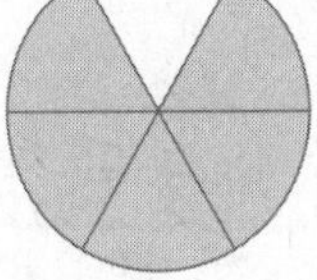

In a fraction, the first (or top) number is called the **numerator**; the second (or bottom) number is called the **denominator**. In the fraction ⅚, the numerator is 5 and the denominator is 6. For fractions with the same denominator, addition and subtraction are easily performed. For example, ⅑ + ⁴⁄₉ represents one of nine, added to four of nine, which is thus five of nine, ⁵⁄₉. In general, for fractions with the same denominator, we can ignore the denominator and focus on the numerators. In other words, to add or subtract fractions with the same denominator, add or subtract the numerators, leaving the denominators unchanged.

The situation is more complicated when we deal with fractions with differing denominators. For example, ½ + ⅓:

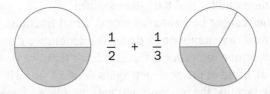

$$\frac{1}{2} + \frac{1}{3}$$

To represent the result as a single fraction, we need to find a way to represent both fractions so that there is an equal number of total pieces in each of the fractions we wish to add. This process is called **finding a common denominator**.

One way to do this (but not always the easiest) is to multiply the two denominators. In this case, the product of the denominators, 2 times 3, is 6. If we cut the pie on the left into six equal pieces instead of two, three of these pieces will equal one-half the pie. On the right, two pieces that are each one-sixth of the pie will equal one-third the pie. The sum therefore is $5/6$:

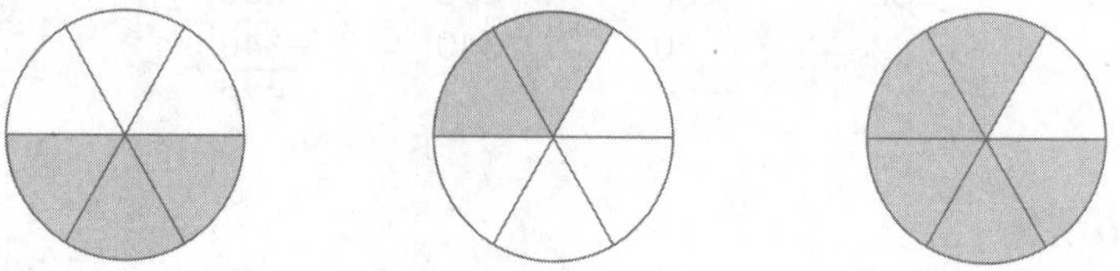

$$\frac{3}{6} + \frac{2}{6} = \frac{5}{6}$$

Notice that $1/2$ represents the same fraction as $3/6$. These two fractions are considered equivalent. In general, two fractions are **equivalent** if you can obtain one from the other by multiplying both the numerator and denominator by the same number:

$$\frac{2}{3} = \frac{2}{3} * \frac{2}{2} = \frac{4}{6} = \frac{4}{6} * \frac{2}{2} = \frac{8}{12} = \frac{8}{12} * \frac{2}{2} = \frac{16}{24}, \text{ etc.}$$

In this example, $2/3$, $4/6$, $8/12$, . . . , are all equivalent.

DECIMALS AND PERCENTAGES

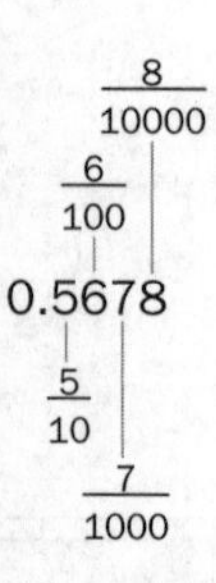

The use of decimals provides a convenient way of representing fractions with denominators that are powers of 10: $1/10$, $3/100$, $72/1000$, for example. **Decimal fractions** are numbers that include a whole part (which may be zero) and a fractional part, separated by a decimal point. In our positional number system (base 10), the place value of each digit *increases* by a power of 10 as we move from right to left. If we move from left to right, the place value *decreases* by a power of 10. This is true of decimal fractions, also. In the number 0.5678, 5 represents tenths, 6 hundredths, 7 thousandths, and 8 ten-thousandths.

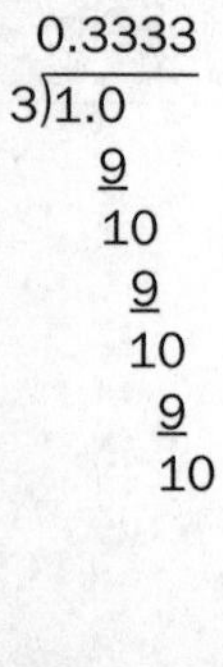

Some fractions cannot be written as nice decimal fractions. Consider $1/3$, for example. To convert this number to a decimal fraction, we carry out long division. We could continue the process forever: Each time we divide 10 by 3, we get a remainder of 1 and in the next step again divide 3 into 10.

To denote the fact that the process continues, we place a bar above the part of the decimal that repeats. In other words, $1/3 = 0.\overline{3}$. In most cases, we are willing to settle for an approximation, but we need to decide how good an approximation. We can specify this by giving the number of *significant digits*. All digits are considered significant except a zero in the left-most position. Thus: to three significant digits, $\frac{1}{3} = 0.333$; to four significant digits, $\frac{1}{3} = 0.3333$. Unfortunately, it is not always this easy. To correctly approximate a decimal number to n significant digits, you must round the nth digit if the next digit to the right is 5 or greater. For example, 2.3456 rounded to three significant digits is 2.346.

Decimal numbers are often reported as *percentages*. To convert a decimal number to a percentage, multiply the number by 100 (move the decimal two places to the right) and add the percent sign, %. For example, 7.25 represents the same value as 725%. To convert a percentage to a decimal, divide the number by 100 (move the decimal two places to the left) and delete the percent sign. For example, 33% is 0.33.

SCIENTIFIC NOTATION

Scientific notation enables us to write down in compact form numbers that often occur in scientific calculations but that are extremely unwieldy when written in the usual form. For example, 0.0000000000001 centimeter is the diameter of the nucleus of an atom. A number in **scientific notation** is written as a decimal number between 1 and 10 multiplied by a power of 10.

There are two simple rules pertaining to interpreting 10 raised to an exponent. First, if the exponent is positive, it tells you how many zeros follow the one. For example, 10^2 is one followed by two zeros (100). Second, if the exponent is negative, it tells you how many places there are to the right of the decimal point. For example, 10^{-3} has three digits to the right of the decimal (0.001).

Here are some examples of how scientific notation can simplify the notation used to describe very large and very small numbers:

- **Avogadro's Number** (the number of molecules in one mole):

  602,213,670,000,000,000,000,000, or $6.0221367 * 10^{23}$

- **Speed of Light:**

  299,792,500 m/s, or $2.997925 * 10^8$ m/s

- **Mass of an Electron:**

  0.00000000000000000000000000000091091 kg, or $9.1091 * 10^{-31}$ kg

To express 5,345,000,000 in scientific notation, we must write this number as 5.345 times some power of 10. To find the proper power of 10, note that the decimal place must be moved nine places to the left. Thus, $5,345,000,000 = 5.345 * 10^9$.

Multiplying very large or very small numbers can be tedious, but the job becomes much easier if the numbers are expressed in scientific notation: To multiply powers of 10, just add the exponents. Suppose we wish to find the product of 31,000,000 times 120,000. That is, we want to evaluate 31,000,000 * 120,000. In scientific notation, this becomes:

$$(3.1 * 10^7) * (1.2 * 10^5)$$

To perform the multiplication, multiply the first numbers: 3.1 * 1.2, which gives 3.72. Then multiply the powers of 10 by adding the exponents: 7 + 5 = 12. Thus:

$$(3.1 * 10^7) * (1.2 * 10^5) = 3.72 * 10^{12}$$

ALGEBRA

Algebra consists of the same operations and rules as arithmetic, but where arithmetic operates on specific numbers, **algebra** operates on variables that can represent many different numbers: It is the language we use to describe patterns and relationships between quantities. When you do a calculation with numbers, you're doing arithmetic; when you use variables to describe how the calculation would be done with numbers, you're doing algebra. If you have a single calculation to complete, you use arithmetic. But if you have many similar calculations to do, you use algebra to describe exactly how the calculations are to be done, thereby reducing both the number and complexity of the steps involved.

Before we can make the transition from arithmetic to algebra, we need to agree upon what we mean by a variable. In common English, "variable" means changeable—anything that varies or changes, something with no fixed value. In mathematics, the term **variable** is used to denote either a quantity that may have a number of different values or the symbol used to denote these values. More specifically, it represents any particular value chosen from a set of values. The set of values that a variable may assume is called the *domain* of the variable. For example, if the domain of the variable x is given as {1,3,4}, then the expression $2 * x$ can take on any of the values we obtain by replacing x with 1, 3, or 4—that is, 2, 6, or 8. When we use variables in a calculation, we are showing how the arithmetic could be done with any of the values in the domain of the variable.

Consider the method we use to multiply two fractions. We can express the rule in words: "To multiply two fractions, multiply the two numerators to get the numerator of the product. Next, multiply the two denominators to get the denominator of the product." The same rule, expressed using modern algebra, is:

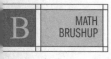

$$\frac{a}{b} * \frac{c}{d} = \frac{a * c}{b * d}$$

The strategy for adding fractions with different denominators can be expressed as:

$$\frac{a}{b} + \frac{c}{d} = \frac{a * d + b * c}{b * d}$$

Reality check: Did you understand what you just read? Did you try substituting values for the variables and verifying the equality? If not, you're not reading the text correctly. Remember, you are reading mathematics now; you should read mathematics with a pencil in your hand.

Technically, we should also give the domain of each of the variables *a, b, c,* and *d,* but today, if no domain is given, then the **default domain** is taken to be the set of numbers for which the statement makes sense. In this case, we can make sense of the expression for any choice of numbers, provided only that the two denominators, *b* and *d,* are nonzero. Thus, the domain of both variables *a* and *c* is all numbers, while the variables *b* and *d* have all nonzero numbers as their domain. (Recall that any expression with a zero in a denominator is undefined: It has no meaning. Consider ³⁄0, for example. It makes no sense to think of this as the result of dividing a unit measure into zero pieces and taking three of them. Nor can we meaningfully interpret what we might mean by the number of times that 0 goes into 3.)

Some Rules of Algebra

So far, we have denoted multiplication by ∗ as is common for most computer applications. When one works with variables, it is more common to denote multiplication by juxtaposition. That is, you simply put the two variables to be multiplied next to each other. For example, $a * b$ is also denoted by ab. A further simplification is **exponents**, numerical superscripts that indicate a variable or number is to be multiplied by itself. For example, $3 * 3$ is denoted by 3^2; $3 * 3 * 3$ by 3^3; $3 * 3 * 3 * 3$ by 3^4; and so on. The number 3^2 is referred to as "three squared," 3^3 as "three cubed." After that, we say "three to the fourth power," "three to the fifth," and so on. Notice this is the same convention used in scientific notation when describing powers of 10.

The language of algebra has evolved over thousands of years, developing a precise format and a specific order in which operations must be performed. Consider $2 * 3 + 5$. This could mean multiply 2 and 3, giving 6, and add 5, giving 11. Alternatively, it could mean add 3 and 5, giving 8, and multiply by 2, giving 16. A decision is needed to settle which of these operations, the multiplication or the addition, should be done first. Similarly, $3 * 2^2$ could mean multiply 3 by 2 to obtain 6, and then square this, giving 36. Alternatively, it could mean square 2, giving 4, and then multiply by 3 to obtain 12. In order to decide such questions, mathematics resorts to the conventions described below.

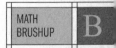
MATH BRUSHUP   B

The Order of Operations

The order of operations is as follows:

1. Parenthetical expressions
2. Exponents
3. Multiplication and division from left to right
4. Additions and subtractions from left to right

Parentheses are used to show which operations should be completed first. If you have several sets of parentheses, the convention is that you start with the innermost and work outward. For example, $14 - (20 - (5+3))$ means that you add the 5 and the 3 first, giving 8; then subtract that from 20, giving 12; finally, subtract that from 14, giving 2.

To simplify the expression $\dfrac{(2 * 3^2 - 8)}{5}$, we begin with the exponent, replacing 3^2 with 9. The next step is to multiply 2 by 9 to get 18. Then we subtract 8 to get 10, divide by 5 to get 2, and finally, add 2 for a total of 4. Algebraically:

$$\frac{(2*3^2-8)}{5} + 2 = \frac{(2*9-8)}{5} + 2 = \frac{(18-8)}{5} + 2 = \frac{10}{5} + 2 = 2 + 2 = 4$$

A word of caution: Mathematics is a precise language—no other language allows us to communicate complex ideas with such specificity. Unfortunately, this precision makes constructing good mathematical sentences very difficult. Of particular importance is the equals symbol (=). Be very careful how you use this symbol. When the equals symbol appears between two expressions, it means they are *identical*. Don't use the symbol unless you are asserting that the expressions on each side of it are *exactly* the same.

Negative Numbers

As we have seen, the first numbers used were the counting, or whole, numbers—1, 2, 3, etc.—then ratios of these numbers, or fractions. Much later, zero was added to the whole numbers, giving the set we now call the natural numbers $\{0, 1, 2, 3 \dots\}$. As trading became more common, whole numbers were needed for two distinctly different uses: to indicate both credits or gains and debts or losses. Conventions were developed to permit the use of whole numbers in both cases. The ancient Chinese, for example, used red for credits and black for debits—exactly the opposite convention from the one we now use.

Early algebraists found that certain equations had no solutions among the natural numbers or fractions. For example, the equation $2 + x = 1$ has no solution

B   MATH BRUSHUP

in the natural numbers. A good way to think of negative numbers is as trick numbers that turn addition into subtraction. For example, $2 - 1 = 1$, so $x = -1$ is considered a solution of $2 + x = 1$. When we try to add -1 to 2, we really end up subtracting 1.

For centuries, there was no practical need for negative numbers, and they were looked upon as little more than mathematical curiosities. It's easy enough to understand what is meant by 3 trees or 5 flowers, but what is meant by -3 trees or -5 flowers?

Using negative numbers in applications is convenient because by using negative numbers, we do not have to consider addition and subtraction as two different operations; rather, we can consider them as examples of a single operation acting in one of two directions. Thus, instead of the natural numbers and two operations, we now use the natural numbers together with their negatives: a set of numbers we call the **integers** (for example: $-2, -1, 0, 1, 2$).

Once we have allowed negative numbers, we can allow fractions with negative numerators and denominators using the following convention:

$$\frac{-a}{b} = -\frac{a}{b} = \frac{a}{-b}$$

The set of numbers that can be written as fractions with integer numerator and denominator, with denominator nonzero, is called the **rational numbers**.

THE NUMBER LINE

The rational numbers have a natural geometric interpretation as points on a ruler. Choose any point on a line segment, then set the distance between the left end and that point as a unit length. Now, mark off units of this length along the line. Each of these marks represents an integer. The value assigned to each mark increases by one as we move to the right. Fractions with the denominator q are then represented by the points that divide each of the unit intervals into q equal parts:

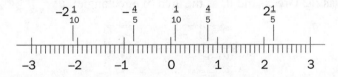

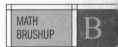

MATH
BRUSHUP   B

Addition and subtraction have a nice geometric interpretation on the number line. To add two numbers, start at the first number, then move the second number of units to the right. For example, to find the sum of -2 and 3, start at -2 on the line above and move 3 units to the right to obtain 1 as the solution. Subtraction is carried out similarly except we move to the left instead of the right. For example, to solve $3 - 4$, we start at 3 and then move 4 units to the left to obtain -1 as the solution.

Given any two points on the line, we consider the one farthest to the right to be the larger of the two. This relationship is expressed with an inequality. If a is to the right of b on the number line, we say $a > b$ (read a is greater than b), or $b < a$ (read b is less than a). Note, if $a > b$, then $-a < -b$. A good way to remember this fact is as the rule: Multiplying both sides of an inequality by -1 reverses the sign.

Unfortunately, as the ancient Greeks discovered, there are lengths that cannot be represented by rational numbers. In order to identify numbers with a continuous line, we are forced to accept the existence of additional numbers, the so-called irrational numbers. **Irrational numbers** are exactly those numbers, not representable as fractions, that are required to make the correspondence between numbers and line segments complete. If the solution to a particular problem involves an irrational number, we approximate it by choosing a fraction close to it. (Note that "close" is a relative term and, in general, requires you to know the purpose of the approximation.)

THE REAL NUMBER SYSTEM

When we consider not only the set of numbers that forms the real line but also the algebraic operations, we are considering not just a set, but a number system. Just as we need only addition to carry out both addition and subtraction, we need only multiplication to carry out both multiplication and division. As we have pointed out, this is exactly how the Babylonians worked with fractions (3 divided by 2 is the same as 3 times $\frac{1}{2}$).

The **real number system** consists of a set of numbers that we can identify with a continuous line—and that therefore includes both rational and irrational numbers—and the operations of addition and multiplication. The correspondence between the real numbers and the number line allows us to visualize both operations. Addition is movement to the right when adding a positive number and to the left when adding a negative; multiplication of positive numbers is visualized as the Greeks did it, as the area of a rectangle:

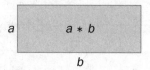

To extend the analogy to negative numbers, find the product of the corresponding positive numbers and then take the negative of the result if one and only one of the numbers is negative. For example, to multiply $-5 * 7$, we draw the rectangle corresponding to $5 * 7$ and then take the negative of the result. If both the numbers are negative, ignore both minus signs. The product of two negative numbers is always a positive number.

The modern way of looking at addition and multiplication is as **operators**—functions that take in a pair of real numbers and produce another real number according to certain rules or properties. The following list of five properties is the shortest possible list needed to define the operations of addition and multiplication on the set of real numbers. As usual, *a, b,* and *c* stand for any real numbers for which the expression makes sense.

Commutative Property

The **commutative property** says that the order in which we perform either addition or multiplication does not matter; the result will be the same:

Addition | Multiplication
$a + b = b + a$ | $a * b = b * a$

When you are trying to understand an algebraic expression, it is always a good idea to substitute numbers for variables. For example:

$5 + 3 = 8$ and $3 + 5 = 8$ | $3 * 4 = 12$ and $4 * 3 = 12$

To better understand what an expression says, it is often useful to justify it geometrically. For example, the commutative property for addition says that if one starts at point *a* on the number line and moves a distance *b,* one ends up at the same point as when one starts at *b* and moves distance *a.* (Try it with some numbers!) The commutative property for multiplication says that the area of a rectangle with sides of length *a* and *b* is the same as the area of a rectangle with sides of length *b* and *a.*

Associative Property

The **associative property** says that, when performing a sequence of additions or a sequence of multiplications, we may choose to begin the sequence from either the right or left end of the expression:

Addition | Multiplication
$(a + b) + c = a + (b + c)$ | $a * (b * c) = (a * b) * c$

For example:

$(2 + 7) + 3 = 9 + 3 = 12$ | $2 * (3 * 5) = 2 * 15 = 30$

and | and

$2 + (7 + 3) = 2 + 10 = 12$ | $(2 * 3) * 5 = 6 * 5 = 30$

MATH BRUSHUP B

See if you can justify the associative property for addition geometrically for yourself. To justify the associative property for multiplication we consider the volume of a rectangular solid with base area $b * c$ of height *a.* This solid has the same volume as the solid with rectangular base $a * b$ of height *c.*

Identity Properties

ADDITION. There is a real number 0 such that $a - 0 = 0 + a = a$.

MULTIPLICATION. There is a real number 1 such that $a * 1 = 1 * a = a$.

Inverse Properties

ADDITION. For each real number a, there is a single real number $-a$ such that:

$$a + (-a) = (-a) + a = 0$$

MULTIPLICATION. For each nonzero real number a, there is a single real number $1/a$ such that:

$$a * \left(\frac{1}{a}\right) = \left(\frac{1}{a}\right) * a = 1$$

Distributive Property

So far, each of the properties we have considered was stated separately for addition and multiplication; the **distributive property** tells us how the two operations interact. Suppose we wish to make sense of the expression $a * (b + c)$. The order of operations tell us that we must add b and c before we multiply by a. However, if we need to do the multiplication first, such as when simplifying the expression $2 * (x - 3)$, the distributive property shows us how this may be done:

$$a * (b + c) = a * b + a * c$$

and

$$(b + c) * a = b * a + c * a$$

For example:

$$3 * (2 + 5) = 3 * 7 + 21$$

and

$$3 * 2 + 3 * 5 = 6 + 15 = 21$$

Also:

$$(4 + 1) * 6 = 5 * 6 = 30$$

and

$$4 * 6 + 1 * 6 = 24 + 6 = 30$$

B   MATH
BRUSHUP

Be sure to draw the pictures to interpret the distributive law geometrically. The ancient Greeks used the technique to great advantage. For example, consider the more complicated identity:

$$(a + b)^2 = a^2 + 2ab + b^2$$

We can establish this identity algebraically using the distributive law:

$$
\begin{aligned}
(a + b)^2 &= (a + b) * (a + b) \\
&= a * (a + b) + b * (a + b) \text{ (once)} \\
&= a^2 + ab + ba + b^2 \text{ (twice)} \\
&= a^2 + 2ab + b^2
\end{aligned}
$$

However, to understand the identity, draw pictures. In Book II of his *Elements*, Euclid established the identity by considering the following diagram:

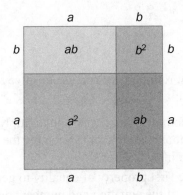

The large square has sides of length $(a + b)$, so the area of the large square is:

$$(a + b)^2$$

This area is equal to the sum of the areas of the four smaller rectangles:

$$a^2 + ab + ab + b^2$$

EXPRESSIONS AND EQUATIONS

MATH
BRUSHUP   B

An algebraic **expression** is a collection of numbers, variables, and symbols for operations, together with symbols for grouping. An **equation** is a statement that two expressions are equivalent. For example, $3x + 1$ is an expression, while $3x + 1 = 2$ is an equation. When we write an equation, we are asserting that the expression on the right side of the equals sign is in every way equivalent to the expression on the left. How do addition and multiplication affect an equation? This question is answered by the following properties.

Properties of Equality

1. We can add or subtract a number from both sides of an equation. Let A and B be algebraic expressions and c any real number. Then:

   $A = B$ if and only if $A + c = B + c$

   For example:

   $y - 3 = 2x + 5$ if and only if $y = 2x + 8$

2. We can multiply both sides of an equation by a nonzero number and preserve the equality. If c is nonzero, then:

   $A = B$ if and only if $c * A = c * B$

   For example:

   $2x = 3$ if and only if $x = 3/2$

Linear Equations

There are many different routines one can use to solve a **linear equation**. Here is one three-step method:

1. Clear parentheses, combine like terms, and multiply both sides of the equation by a common denominator (preferably the least common denominator) to eliminate fractions.
2. Use addition and the first property of equality to get a multiple of the variable on one side of the equation and numbers only on the other.
3. Use multiplication and the second property of equality to solve for the variable.

For example, suppose we wish to solve the equation $2(x + 2) = 3x - 1$. We first clear the parentheses by distributing the 2: $2x + 4 = 3x - 1$. Next, we subtract $2x$ from both sides of the equation to obtain $4 = x - 1$. Finally, we add 1 to both sides to find the solution, $x = 5$.

Consider the slightly more complicated equation $3x + ⅔ = 2(x - ¼) + 2$. Following step 1, we distribute the 2 on the right-hand side of the equation to obtain:

$$3x + \frac{2}{3} = 2x - \frac{5}{2} + 2$$

Combining like terms, we have:

$$3x + \frac{2}{3} = 2x - \frac{1}{2}$$

The least common denominator of the two fractions is 6. Multiplying both sides by 6 yields:

$$18x + 4 = 12x - 3$$

Following step 2, we subtract $12x$ from both sides and subtract 4 from both sides. The result is:

$$6x = -7$$
$$x = -\frac{7}{6}$$

It is always a good idea to check your solution by substituting it into the original equation. If we substitute $x = -\frac{7}{6}$ into the original equation, we obtain:

$$\frac{-21}{6} + \frac{2}{3} = 2\left(\frac{-7}{6} - \frac{5}{4}\right) + 2$$

or

$$\frac{-17}{6} = \frac{-17}{6}$$

confirming the validity of our solution.

PRIME NUMBERS AND FACTORING

A **prime number** is a whole number larger than 1 that is divisible only by 1 and itself. Every whole number can be written as a product of prime factors. Factoring, reducing fractions, and simplifying algebraic expressions all require a knowledge of prime numbers. Here are some helpful hints to determine divisibility by 2, 3, 5, or 9:

- All even numbers are divisible by 2.
- A number is divisible by 3 if the sum of its digits is divisible by 3.
- A number is divisible by 5 if its last digit is 5 or 0.
- A number is divisible by 9 if the sum of its digits is divisible by 9.

For example, if we wish to factor 1,122, we know that 3 is a factor because the sum of the digits is 6. Dividing 1,122 by 3 yields 374. Because 374 is even, we know that 2 is a factor of it. Thus, $1{,}122 = 3 * 2 * 187$. To factor 187 takes a little effort, but after a bit of guessing, you should find that $11 * 17 = 187$. Thus, $1{,}122 = 3 * 2 * 11 * 17$.

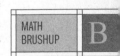

To factor 128, we note that it is even. In fact, $128 = 2 * 64$, 64 is even, and $64 = 2 * 32$. Continuing, we have:

$$128 = 2 * 64 = 2^2 * 32 = 2^2 * (2 * 16) = 2^3 * (2 * 8) = 2^4 * (2 * 4) =$$
$$2^5 * (2 * 2) = 2^7$$

WORKING WITH EXPONENTS

Let x stand for any real number, and let n be a positive integer. By x^n or $x^{\wedge}n$, we mean x multiplied by itself n times:

$$x^n = x * x * \ldots * x$$
$$(n \text{ multiples of } x)$$

For example,

$$3^2 = 3 * 3 = 9 \ \textit{and} \ 3^5 = 3 * 3 * 3 * 3 * 3 = 243$$

There are three basic rules for manipulating exponents; they are often called the **laws of exponents.** Rather than memorize them as formal rules, understand them as consequences of the above notation, and you will always be able to re-create them when needed.

The First Law of Exponents

The first law concerns expressions of the form $x^m * x^n$. Now:

$$x^m * x^n = (x * \ldots * x) * (x * \ldots * x)$$
$$(m \text{ multiples}) \quad (n \text{ multiples})$$

As we have a total of $m + n$ multiples of x:

$$x^m * x^n = x^{m+n}$$

For example:

$$2^5 * 2^4 = 2^9$$

and

$$5^2 * 5^3 = 5^5$$

Notice, if we choose $m = 0$ in the above law, we obtain:

$$x^0 * x^n = x^n$$

Look closely at the form of this equation. We have x^0 multiplied by x^n equal to x^n. Since this statement is true for all real numbers x and positive integers n, x^0 must be the multiplicative identity. In other words, for the notation x^0 to make sense, x^0 must be equal to 1. Hence, any number raised to the zero power is equal to 1. Thus, for example, $2^0 = 1$.

The Second Law of Exponents

The second law of exponents concerns expression of the form $(x^n)^m$. Here, as is often the case, the parentheses tell us to view x^n as a single number. Thus, the form of the expression is some number raised to the mth power. For example:

$$(x^2)^3 = (x^2) * (x^2) * (x^2) = (x * x) * (x * x) * (x * x) = x * x * x * x * x * x = x^6$$

In general,

$$(x^n)^m = x^n * \ldots * x^n \; (m \; multiples \; of \; x^n)$$

Expanding each x^n:

$$= (x * \ldots \ldots * x) * \ldots * (x * \ldots \ldots * x) \; (m \; sets \; of \; parentheses$$
$$= x^{n} *{}^{m} \; (n * m \; multiples \; of \; x) \; each \; with \; n \; multiples \; of \; x)$$

Now that we realize $x^{n\,*\,m}$ is just shorthand for $n * m$ x's multiplied together, it is easy to see that we can also group the x's into n sets, each with m multiples of x. Therefore:

$$x^{n\,*\,m} = (x^n)^m = (x^m)^n$$

Several other rules can be derived immediately from the notation in this way. In particular, if a and b are any real numbers:

$$(a * b)^n = (a * b) * \ldots * (a * b) \; (n \; multiples \; of \; a * b)$$
$$= (a * \ldots * a) * (b * \ldots * b) \; (n \; multiples \; of \; a) * (n \; multiples \; of \; b)$$
$$= a^n * b^n$$

and provided $b \neq 0$:

$$\left(\frac{a}{b}\right)^n = \left(\frac{a}{b}\right) * \ldots * \left(\frac{a}{b}\right) \; (n \; multiples \; of \; ab)$$

$$= \frac{(a * \ldots * a)}{(b * \ldots * b)} \; (n \; multiples \; of \; a \div n \; multiples \; of \; b)$$

$$= \frac{a^n}{b^n}$$

For example:

$$\left(\frac{3}{2}\right)^n = \frac{3^2}{2^2} = \frac{9}{4}$$

The Third Law of Exponents

The third law involves one more notational convention. The multiplicative reciprocal of a number x is denoted by $1/x$ or x^{-1}. Thus, $3^{-1} = 1/3$ and $5^{-1} = 1/5$ How should we make sense of an expression like x^{-n}? According to the second law:

$$x^{-n} = (x^{-1})^n = \left(\frac{1}{x}\right)^n = \frac{1^n}{x^n} = \frac{1}{x^n}$$

It is useful to remember that this last expression remains true even when n is negative. With $-k$ in place of n, the last expression, in reverse order, is:

$$\frac{1}{x^{-k}} = x^{-(-k)} = x^k$$

Consider the expression x^7/x^2. We can simplify this expression using the cancellation law:

$$\frac{x^7}{x^2} = \frac{x^2}{x^2} * \frac{x^5}{1} = \frac{x^5}{1} = x^5$$

In general, take m and n positive integers; consider x^n/x^m. In the numerator of this fraction, we have x multiplied by itself n times, while in the denominator, we have x multiplied by itself m times. Using the cancellation law, we can cancel m x's to obtain:

$$\frac{x^n}{x^m} = \frac{\overbrace{(x * \ldots * x)}^{(m\ \text{multiples})} * \overbrace{(x * \ldots * x)}^{[(n-m)\ \text{multiples}]}}{\underbrace{(x * \ldots * x)}_{(m\ \text{multiples})}} = \frac{x^m}{x^m} * x^{n-m} = x^{n-m}$$

For example:

$$\frac{2^3}{2^{-7}} = 2^{3-(-7)} = 2^{10}$$

and

$$\frac{3^4}{3^5} = 3^{4-5} = 3^{-1} = \frac{1}{3}$$

Nth Roots and Rational Exponents

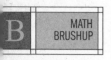

Suppose that a and b are two positive real numbers and that $a^n = b$. In this case, we say that a is an nth root of b. We express this by writing $b(1/n) = a$ or $a = \sqrt[n]{b}$. With this notational convention, we can assign meaning to $a(p/q)$ for any positive integers a, p, and q. We interpret $a(p/q)$ as $(a^p)^{1/q}$ or equivalently $(a^{1/q})^p$. For example:

$$9^{\frac{3}{2}} = (9^{\frac{1}{2}})^3 = (\sqrt[2]{9})^3 = 3^3 = 27$$

RATIOS

A **ratio** is a measure of one quantity relative to the other. Consider the following two lines:

If our goal is to compare the length of one line segment to that of the other, it is natural to use the length of the smaller segment as a unit of measure and ask, "How many of the smaller does it take to make up the larger?"

As the figure illustrates, it takes three of the shorter line segments to equal the length of the longer. We describe the situation by saying that the longer line segment is three times as long as the shorter or that the ratio of the longer to the shorter is 3 to 1.

Suppose we wish to compare the size of California's population to that of Oregon's. According to the 2000 census, California was home to 33,871,648 people, while 3,421,399 persons resided in Oregon. Clearly, many more people call California home than Oregon. Computing the ratio of California's population to Oregon's gives $33{,}871{,}648/3{,}421{,}399 = 9.89$. This tells us that California's population is roughly 10 times as big as Oregon's.

Another instance in which ratios play an important role is in discussing changes in a quantity over time. For example, in 1950 the Earth's population was 2.6 billion; by 2000, it had grown to 6.1 billion. We can describe the situation by describing the net gain in humans, which is 3.5 billion ($6.1 - 2.6$). Or, instead of computing the difference of the two populations, we may take their ratio. We obtain $6.1/2.6$, or 2.3461. This tells us that the population grew by a factor of 2.3; that is, it is now more than twice the size it was in 1950.

Yet another way to describe the change is as **relative change,** the ratio of the change in size to the original size.

$$\text{Relative Change} = \frac{\text{Change in Size}}{\text{Original Size}} = \frac{\text{New Size} - \text{Original Size}}{\text{Original Size}}$$
$$= \frac{\text{New Size}}{\text{Original Size}} - 1$$

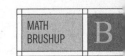

MATH BRUSHUP — B

In comparing the two world populations, we calculate the relative change as:

$$\frac{6.1}{2.6} - 1 = 2.3461 - 1 = 1.3461$$

Relative change is often expressed as a percentage. The origin of the term "percent" reveals the meaning: per cent, or per hundred. To express the relative change in the Earth's population between 1950 and 2000 as a percentage, we express 1.3461 as a fraction with denominator equal to 100. That is, we multiply by 100 to obtain 134.61 percent. In other words, the Earth's population increased by almost 135 percent over the 50 years from 1950 to 2000.

To convert a fraction expressed in decimal form to a percentage, simply multiply by 100. Conversely, to convert a percentage to a decimal form, divide by 100. For example:

$$1.13\% = 0.0113$$

and

$$425\% = 4.25$$

More generally:

$$a \text{ is } p\% \text{ of } b \text{ means } a = \frac{p}{100} * b$$

Thus:

$$5.5 \text{ percent of } 22 \text{ is } \left(\frac{5.5}{100}\right) * 22 = 1.21$$

People use percentages in several different ways, depending on what they want to show. For example, a store may report that it uses a 50-percent markup on its wares. This would lead you to believe that, if the store pays $20 for an item, you might purchase it for 50 percent more, or $30. More generally, if the store paid x dollars, you would pay $x + 0.5x = 1.5x$. In fact, this may not be the case. When the store reports its markup, it means that 50 percent of the price you pay is markup. In other words, if the store pays x dollars, it sells the item for $2x$ dollars. It doubles the price so the relative change is 1, which corresponds to a relative increase of 100 percent, not 50 percent.

A similar misleading use of percentages is employed by the major oil companies. Instead of reporting profits as a percentage of their investment, they report their profits as a percentage of their sales. Thus, if an oil company puts up an original investment of $10 million, which leads to sales of $40 million and net profits of $2 million, it says that its profit is:

$$\frac{\$2 \text{ million}}{\$40 \text{ million}} = 0.05 \text{ or } 5\%$$

Calculating the profit as a return on investment, however, we find that:

$$\frac{\$2 \text{ million}}{\$40 \text{ million}} = 0.20 \text{ or } 20\%$$

A METHOD FOR DEALING WITH WORD PROBLEMS*

There is no single method for dealing with word problems; however, the following steps should serve as a general guide:

1. Read the problem over first quickly to get an idea of what it's about; then read it again *very* carefully. Make sure you have a clear idea of what every sentence means and why each word is there. In your mind's eye, get as vivid a picture as possible—it really helps to see what is going on in the problem!
2. Decide what the question is asking you to find. Let a variable represent it.
3. Draw a picture if appropriate. On it, mark any lengths, distances, etc., that are given in the problem or that can be expressed in terms of the variable.
4. Write down *in words* an equation connecting the various quantities in the problem. This equation is usually hidden in, or implied by, the wording of the problem. If you can't see it, read the problem again carefully. Look for any wording in the problem that tells you how one quantity is related to another.
5. List any formulas that might help.
6. Write the equations in symbols, by expressing the unknown quantities in terms of the variable and substituting any numerical values given in the problem.
7. Using substitution, write an equation in one variable.
8. Solve the equation.
9. Check that your solution is reasonable from a commonsense point of view and that it satisfies the conditions of the problem.

Let's apply this method to the following problem:

Find a number whose double is 8 more than the result of subtracting the original number from 25.

Go through the steps outlined above. Here are the relevant ones for this problem:

Step 2. The problem is asking you to find a number, so let the number be x.
Step 4. The equation comes from the fact that:

Double of x = 8 more than the result of subtracting x from 25

Step 5. To double a number, you multiply it by 2.

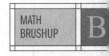
MATH BRUSHUP B

*Adapted from Deborah Huges-Hallet, *The Math Workshop*. New York: Norton, 1980.

Step 6. The double of x is $2x$.

Step 7. Substituting these expressions into the equation in step 4 yields:

$$2x = (25 - x) + 8$$

Step 8. Solving the equation results in:

$$3x = 33$$
$$x = 11$$

Step 9. Check:

- Double of x is 22.
- Subtracting x from 25 gives 14, and 8 more than 14 is 22.
- Therefore, 11 is the answer to the problem.

FINANCING
YOUR EDUCATION

One obstacle on the road to a college career may be money. College for an adult learner is an expense that often does not factor into a family's budget.

Besides tuition, which varies from college to college, you may incur the following expenses:

- application fee, which ranges from $25 to $75 or more
- books and supplies, which may run from $60 to several hundred dollars per course
- parking and transportation fees
- student activities fee, which often allows you to use the recreational facilities, counseling services, and public areas of the college
- laboratory fee
- computer laboratory fee
- library fee
- baby-sitting costs, if you need to provide child care while you attend school
- photocopying costs for your own research
- costs for residencies if required as part of a distance learning program

An advisor at the college can help you assess which fees are applicable to your program. Remember that continuing your education may result in greater employment opportunities; therefore, an investment in your education usually pays you back.

A SSESSING YOUR COLLEGE EXPENSES

To assess your own college expenses, fill in the appropriate columns on this worksheet. In the second column, write down the cost of the item. In the third column, indicate the available funds to pay for the item. Record the funds you still need to cover each item in the fourth column.

ITEM NEEDED	COST	FUNDS AVAILABLE	FUNDS NEEDED
application fee			
tuition (cost per credit or per course)			
books			
parking and transportation fees			
activities fee			
laboratory fee			
computer laboratory fee			
library fee			
baby-sitting costs			
personal office supplies (paper, pens, notebooks)			
additional expenses (computer, printer, calculator, etc.)			
others:			
Totals:			

C

HOW TO FIND FINANCIAL AID

College catalogues and Web sites will give you an overview of the financial aid possibilities offered to adult students. These include:

- tuition payment plans
- reimbursement from your employer
- federal and state loans and grants
- local scholarships (sponsored by community groups, businesses, religious organizations, and public service organizations)
- school-sponsored scholarships and grants

Many colleges have a financial aid officer to help sort through the many possibilities available for financing your education. Because federal financial aid guidelines change every year, it is important that you work closely with your financial aid officer so that you get the most up-to-date information.

SCHOLARSHIPS AND GRANTS

Scholarships and grants do not have to be repaid. They are awarded for financial need and/or academic merit. These forms of financial aid usually require separate applications, sometimes including letters of recommendation or personal essays. The following publications (often available at local libraries, college libraries, and high school guidance offices) may help you locate a scholarship or grant opportunity:

- *Chronicle Student Aid Manual*
- *Directory of Financial Aid for Minorities*
- *Directory of Financial Aid for Women*
- *Financial Aid for Veterans and Their Dependents*
- *Financial Aid for the Disabled*
- *Scholarships, Fellowships, and Loans*

Because scholarships sometimes target specific recipient groups (second-generation Italian American women, for example), the better informed you are about the offerings, the more likely you are to find a scholarship appropriate to your needs.

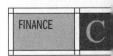

FINANCE   C

LOANS

Loans from the federal government, state government, or banks need to be paid back with interest. The payback period varies according to the loan, as does the interest charged. Students who are considering loans might also want to think about using a home equity line of credit, which allows interest deductions from federal income tax. "The Student Guide: Five Federal Financial Aid Programs" is available free from:

Federal Student Aid Programs
Department L-10
Pueblo, CO 81009-001

ASSISTANTSHIPS, INTERNSHIPS, AND WORK–STUDY PLANS

These programs require that the student work in exchange for tuition benefits or to earn money for college expenses. Assistantships sometimes involve teaching; these opportunities may be available for graduate students. Internships involve learning in the workplace, and work–study plans often involve service on campus.

ONLINE RESOURCES

Financial aid information often is available online through links on a college's Web site. Other useful online sources include

- *www.petersons.com/finaid*
- *www.online-degrees-and-scholarships.com* (contains links to other sources of information)
- *www.geteducated.com*
- *www.ericdigests.org*
- *www.back2college.com/library/finaid.htm*
- *www.collegeboard.org/finaid*

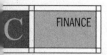

INDEX

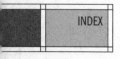
INDEX